#GIRLCODE

#GIRLCODE

THE SECRET TO SUCCESS
IN A DIGITAL WORLD

Michaela Launerts

NEW
HOLLAND

CONTENTS

CHAPTER 7. OUT AND ABOUT - 77

etiquette / *et-ee-kuht* / noun
The customary code of polite behavior in society or among members of a particular profession or group.

INTRODUCTION

This book is a guide to help you develop the confidence you need to become the best version of yourself. What you learn will enable you to interact with all sorts of people without the anxiety and awkwardness that seems to prevent us from achieving our personal goals. In this technological age, competition for employment is fierce. In order to stand out from the crowd, you need to be personable. Ironically, the social media phenomenon has led to a rapid decline in people's social skills. We live in a time where face-to-face contact has been replaced with cyberspace presence and connecting with friends means disconnecting from reality. Sure, the benefits of technology are many, but the damage is, and continues to be, far reaching.

For instance, the more time we spend in an online world, the less time we spend developing basic communication skills that are a critical component of our personal development. So many young people lack the confidence needed to interact in a social setting, let alone in a workplace or job interview. That is why now, more than ever, you need to learn how to behave in contemporary social and professional settings in order to be able to thrive within them. If social skills are the building blocks of confidence and character, then the ability to communicate effectively is the VIP ticket to personal success.

Learning about manners, social graces and conduct will not only enable you to develop confidence, it will make way for the realization that you have the potential to contribute meaningfully to the world and live a happy, fulfilled life. You are the future and if you wish to be taken seriously, you need to understand the intricate mechanisms of the society that exists on this side of the screen. Knowing how to adjust your behavior to suit all sorts of environments and social settings removes a huge amount of pressure and unnecessary anxiety, giving you the space to flourish in any social or professional context. Your actions define you. Don't be imprisoned by uncertainty, be free to explore your potential in the world.

CHAPTER 1

MANNERS

"I have come to believe that our innate purpose is nothing more than to be the greatest version of ourselves. It is a process of refinement, improvement and enhancement. When you are aligned with this process and living your purpose, you have the potential of creating something amazing."
—Dr. Steve Maraboli

Being well mannered is about acknowledging the needs of others before your own. In other words, making others feel at ease in your company. In all cultures, the behaviors that constitute 'acceptable conduct' form the basis of a social framework for people to operate within. For example, think of society in terms of a game. The rules of the game set the standard needed in order to provide an even playing field. Consciously, or unconsciously, disregarding these widely accepted social rules is generally viewed as bad behavior or etiquette. Most people notice poor behavior when they see it, making it very difficult to get back into the game, that is, to build or repair your reputation as a respected player.

Understanding, refining and practicing good manners will allow you to form a valuable set of skills with which to navigate through any social situation. Once you master these skills, you will begin to develop the confidence needed to achieve personal and professional success.

ACTIONS SPEAK LOUDER THAN WORDS

"The shortest and surest way to live with honor in the world, is to be in reality what we would appear to be; all human virtues increase and strengthen themselves by the practice and experience of them."
—Socrates

Good manners are perceived as an outward demonstration of one's personality. Put simply, if you are the product, then your actions are your marketing team. It is important to practice good manners as it makes your behavior attractive. Not only does this speak volumes about the *quality* of your character but ensures people respond to you in a positive manner throughout your life. Demonstrating attractive behavior is also a vital component in developing your reputation. Think of it as a marketing campaign that will follow you throughout your life. The formula is simple; if you wish to be treated with respect, you must be respectful of others.

"Good manners will open doors that the best education cannot." —
Clarence Thomas

DAILY DO'S AND DON'TS

- Say 'Please' and 'Thank you' whenever necessary.
- Say 'Excuse me' if you bump into somebody or wish to attract attention.
- Sneezing and coughing is acceptable if you cover your mouth with a tissue or handkerchief.
- Avoid burping and passing wind. It is widely regarded as offensive and should be reserved for the bathroom.
- Step to the side when passing someone in a narrow space.
- Respond to greetings appropriately.
- Smile and if somebody smiles at you, smile back.
- Say 'Goodbye' when leaving.
- Stay in your place when queuing.
- Be conscious of others' personal space.
- Don't feel compelled to say everything that comes to your mind.
- Avoid shouting or disrupting others in public.
- Think before you speak; if what you're about to say isn't complimentary, don't say it.
- If a person within a close proximity drops something, pick up the item and return it.
- Apologize immediately if you think you have accidentally offended somebody.

CHAPTER 2

FIRST IMPRESSIONS

"…I tend to make up my mind about people within thirty seconds
of meeting them… I rely far more on gut instinct than
researching huge amounts of statistics."
—*Richard Branson*

IMPORTANCE

We've all heard it, 'You never get a second chance to make a first impression'. For the most part, this is true. People make their minds up relatively quickly when it comes to their initial perceptions of you, so it makes sense that you would go about ensuring you become noticed for the right reasons, rather than the wrong ones. What you don't do is just as important. Your body language, the way you speak and the way you present yourself all work together and reflect a clear message about the sort of person you are so you need to ensure that you are equipped with the knowledge that will enable you to take control of how you are perceived by others.

POSITIVE BODY LANGUAGE

Many people fail to recognize the power of body language. The way you carry yourself reveals a lot about you and has an enormous impact on how you are perceived by other people. Everything you do can be interpreted. While your posture, when standing tall, reflects confidence and pride, slouching can indicate apathy, nonchalance or even low self-esteem. It is important that you become aware of the signals you are sending to others so that you can exercise control over the impressions you make. Aim to keep your body language open by consciously making an effort to keep your arms unfolded, keep your hands out of your pockets and avoid excessively fidgeting.

When walking, it is important to look straight ahead rather than at the ground and always be aware of others' personal space. If you cross paths with another person, it is polite to step to the side so that they may pass by with ease, regardless of their age, status or condition. By remaining alert and attentive to the needs of other people, it is highly likely that you will be perceived in a positive light.

Reading the Body Language of Others. Most people read body language intuitively (whether they realize it or not) and use it to determine whether a person's attitude is positive or negative. This can be detrimental if you are unsure of the signals you are transmitting, especially in a social or professional scenario. Use the following table as a guide to help you monitor your own body language so that you may remain in control of the impression you wish to make.

Body Language/Gesture	Interpretation
Crossed arms	Shy, guarded, closed, angry, frustrated
Rigidity	Nervous, insecure, uncomfortable
Slouching	Nonchalant, apathetic, low self-esteem
Frowning	Sadness, emotional distress
Furrowed brow	Angry, annoyed, frustrated, unpleasant
Scowling	Petulant, angry
Inability to make/hold eye contact	Duplicitous, disingenuous, insincere
Turning your back	Arrogant, dismissive
Ignoring others	Exclusive
Fidgeting	Nervous, bored, anxious
Fetal position	Guarded, anxious, distressed
Twitching or tapping	Nervous, anxious
Staring	Shocked
Whispering	Sneaky
Speaking a language other than the one that is dominant in a group	Duplicitous, intentionally ostracizing
Sneezing, coughing, spluttering without covering your mouth	Disregard for the health of others
Belching or passing wind	Disregard for the comfort of others
Smiling and laughing	Warmth, friendliness, openness, confidence

INTRODUCTIONS

While involving a certain amount of skill, the ability to introduce someone properly in a social situation is well worth the effort in terms of creating a good first impression and making everybody involved feel completely at ease. The more you practice, the easier it will become and the more confident you will appear. It is generally accepted that when introducing people, they are introduced to the person with the highest social status first. Generally speaking, girls are introduced to boys, children are introduced to adults and ladies to men. It is polite to refer to adults by their title (Mr., Mrs., or Ms.) and surname, initially as a sign of respect unless of course they specifically request to be called by their first name. Use phrases such as 'this is' and 'pleased to meet you'. If the occasion calls for a more formal introduction, it is appropriate to use phrases such as 'may I present' and 'how do you do'.

THE HANDSHAKE

A universal greeting, the introductory handshake should be thought of as the icing atop the good impression cake, without it, the cake is bland and will quickly be forgotten. There are a few simple rules when it comes to greeting somebody properly in this manner. Following them will give you the confidence you need to stand out in any situation.

When meeting someone for the first time in a social or professional context it is important to convey warmth, sincerity and confidence. Most employers will actively seek these qualities in a potential employee, which is why so much emphasis is placed on the way we shake hands. If executed correctly, the greeting becomes a physical symbol of the quality of one's character.

Type of Handshake	How it's Received/Interpreted
The Ace: firm, even, smooth, brief	Sincere, honest, enthusiastic, confident, reliable
The Dead Fish: soft, limp or loose	Meek, insipid, self-conscious, shy, disinterested
The Crusher: too firm/ tight	Arrogant, domineering, egotistical, insecure
The Clinger: failure to let go	Weak, overeager, agreeable, insincere
The Sandwich: both hands	Submissive, overeager
The Wet Blanket: sweaty, wet palms	Nervous, anxious, insecure, self-conscious
The Usurper: top of the hand faces upward	Cocky, arrogant, domineering, intimidating, rude

SHAKING HANDS: THE DO'S AND DON'TS

–   Always extend your right hand with your palm facing sideways and your thumb facing upward. Your hands should meet palm to palm and web to web (the area between your thumb and forefinger).
–   Do not twist the other person's hand so that the top of your hand faces upward, this is rude and conveys a sense of superiority.
–   Similarly, avoid extending your arm palm down as this gesture

implies that you expect your hand to be kissed.

- Avoid a loose grip, limp wrist, sweaty palm or jelly arm. These qualities are extremely off-putting in a handshake.
- Two or three smooth pumps is sufficient, you do not want the other person to feel awkward or uncomfortable.
- Remember to let go; over enthusiastic shaking demonstrates a lack of confidence.
- A handshake should be firm, but not aggressive.
- Look the person in the eye and smile.
- Respond to statements such as 'lovely to meet you' with 'likewise'. It is equally important that verbal greetings are reciprocated accordingly.

GENERAL GREETINGS

In social situations you need to use your discretion as greetings may vary according to factors such as familiarity and culture. For instance, when meeting somebody for the first time, kissing and hugging would be far too intimate a gesture and may be considered an invasion of personal space; whereas this may be perfectly acceptable in the company of close relatives. If you take the initiative and extend your hand, however, not only will you appear confident, you will have made the other person feel completely at ease. Consistently making others feel at ease will serve you well in the future by helping you build a good reputation. If you find yourself in a situation where kissing and/ or hugging is culturally or socially appropriate, ensure you apply the following guidelines:

- If kissing is appropriate, avoid actually placing your lips on

a person's face. Cheeks should come into brief contact—the
actual kiss happens in the air.

- Generally, the level of familiarity dictates whether a kiss is
  appropriate. Women tend to kiss women hello and goodbye
  more than men.
- Follow the leader. Be aware that the kisser may attempt to
  kiss both cheeks so be ready to reciprocate. Turning away too
  quickly could make the other person feel awkward if they have
  already attempted the double kiss.
- If somebody attempts to hug you, avoid rigidly holding your
  hands by your side, unless of course you wish to send the fairly
  clear message, never hug me again.
- Unless you know someone intimately, avoid touching after the
  initial handshake. Invading one's personal space may create
  a feeling of discomfort and create unnecessary tension. In
  addition, some gestures may be considered patronizing, rude
  or sexual in nature so avoid the following at all times: patting
  somebody on the head or bottom and caressing of any sort.

CHARACTER AND REPUTATION

*"The way to gain a good reputation is to endeavor
to be what you desire to appear."*
—Socrates

People can be particularly selective when it comes to images of themselves that are made visible to the public online. This is because we have a natural inclination to control how we are perceived by other people. Similarly, our actions in public and the way we present ourselves sends clear messages to those around us about the qualities we possess as individuals.

In the same way that online profiles are built and reshaped by comments, images and conduct in cyberspace, your real-life reputation is developing just as quickly. In both contexts you need to be cautious. Good reputations can take a long time to build and a moment to ruin.

Developing your character simply means regularly practicing being the kind of person you wish to become. Showing initiative, going out of your way for others and taking the time to make those with whom you come into contact feel at ease are simple ways to exercise your character muscle. As it becomes stronger, not only will you be presented with more opportunities, you will also have developed the confidence to take those opportunities. This is because by engaging in positive actions every day, you become outward facing and open to new experiences. Conversely, underdeveloped social skills may result in diminished confidence and inward-facing behavior. In turn, this could draw a person into the false sense of security of using technology as a way of tuning out of real-life situations in which they feel ill equipped to navigate. This vicious cycle is one of the negative aspects of a technological age where being armed with our devices 24 hours a day, can paradoxically lead to anti-social behavior.

CONFIDENCE AND SELF-ESTEEM

It seems strange and incomprehensible, but sometime in the near future, the issues you have now and worry about most, will be the things you laugh hysterically about with your friends later on. It's true. Being considered cool by others requires you to follow a simple formula. First of all you need to like yourself and be confident. If you don't like you, nobody else will. Secondly, you need to start doing whatever it is you like doing. If you're spending your time doing things that you like, people will naturally be drawn to you.

In life, people generally lead, follow or get in the way of the ones trying to lead or follow. Whatever you do, don't get in the way because that's just embarrassing. The great thing about being at this stage in your life is that you get to discover who you are, and the process can be so much fun. If you try to be more like yourself rather than a mixture of everyone else in your group, the likely result will be more friends and more confidence. Sometimes girls will morph into the image of whomever they're dating at the time. For instance, they become obsessed with tanning if their boyfriend surfs, purchase all the black eye-liner they can carry if their boyfriend listens to death-metal music and get piercings everywhere if their boyfriend looks like a Christmas tree, for whatever reason! It's never the other way around because so many girls are too scared about what other people may think of them if they try to be themselves.

Sure, you can't know what flavor you like the best until you've taken a bite out of all the chocolates in the box, but that's the beauty of it all—you become who you are because of the experiences you have along the way. Don't rush, just have more experiences and get to know and like the person you are. Then, all of a sudden you'll find that you have acquired all the acceptance you need to be able to focus on other things... like shoes.

TEN STEPS TO PROJECTING CONFIDENCE

1. Practice good manners.
2. Maintain eye contact with people you speak to.
3. Perfect your handshake.
4. Stand up straight with your shoulders back.
5. Avoid slouching when seated.
6. Hold your head up and look forward rather than at the ground.
7. Take pride in your appearance.
8. Say please and thank you frequently.
9. Avoid fidgeting, arm crossing and other types of closed body language.
10. Demonstrate attractive behavior by being considerate.

"Kindness in words creates confidence. Kindness in thinking creates profoundness. Kindness in giving creates love."
—Lao Tzu

INTERVIEW ETIQUETTE

*"All our dreams can come true, if we have the
courage to pursue them."*
—Walt Disney

Being interviewed is a daunting experience for most people, regardless of age or status. There are however, a few things you can do that will give you an advantage over your competitors. Firstly, to secure an interview, you need to ensure you look good on paper. Use your resume as a tool to persuade the employer that you have the qualities they are looking for. To achieve this, you have to engage in some research. What is the business of the organization? What do they stand for? If you make the effort to find out, you are already setting yourself apart from the crowd by aligning yourself with the ethos of any potential employer. Anything you do to make yourself an attractive candidate for selection will work in your favor.

Secondly, once the interview has been secured, specific steps need to be taken to ensure you meet the other elements of the selection criteria. That is, ensuring that you are perceived as the best person for the role on paper and in reality—regardless of what that role may be. This can be achieved by focusing on three key areas: behavior, appearance and your attitude.

ATTRACTIVE BEHAVIOR

The things we do (action) and fail to do (inaction) are vital elements of non-verbal communication that shape the way we are perceived by others. Therefore, consistently striving to be the best version of ourselves is a key factor in sending out a positive message. It is highly likely that the interviewer has already made up their mind about you, even before you sit down to be interviewed. That is why you need to behave in a manner that reflects excellence from the second you enter an establishment. In fact, the interview process itself merely serves as a means of reinforcing whatever the interviewer already thinks they know about you.

Arriving promptly to any appointment is essential. It conveys enthusiasm and a sense that you acknowledge that time is a precious commodity. If you are late, even by a few minutes, the message you are sending is that you aren't really all that interested in the first place. Something as simple as arriving at an interview on time reflects a positive work ethic, high standards, self-respect and efficiency.

Smile. If you look as though you are happy to be where you are, the message to your potential employer will be positive. Humans are biologically programmed to read facial expressions, if your expression is interpreted as negative or unpleasant, a potential employer's impression of you will be the same.

Alert the appropriate person of your arrival by attracting their attention. Be considerate of their work environment by saying 'excuse me' and stating your purpose before sitting down to wait.

Avoid eating or drinking at this stage, unless of course there is water available. If you need to freshen up or have a drink, do so in the bathroom or before entering the building.

Show initiative and convey the effort you have put into your preparation by sitting up straight and having a copy of your resume to hand. This shows that you have made an effort to ensure the process runs smoothly for all involved.

When your name is called, acknowledge the person by smiling and following them into the interview area. If the person conducting the interview doesn't take the lead and make you feel immediately at ease, you should take it upon yourself to do so by introducing yourself and shaking hands with the person/people in the room before taking your seat.

Organizations that require a vast quantity of personnel such as many of the larger retail chains, may conduct group interviews in which the candidates are assessed for their suitability on a larger scale. If you find yourself in this scenario, the same rules apply in that your aim remains to be noticed for the right reasons. You may be required to participate in small group activities in which your communication skills and ability to work as a part of a team will be observed and recorded.

PROFESSIONAL APPEARANCE

When dressing for a job interview, your goal should be to convey a standard of excellence. This is due to the fact that people equate the amount of effort you put into grooming with the amount of effort you demonstrate in general. When it comes to making a positive impression in an interview, nothing demonstrates a strong work ethic and a personal standard of excellence as effectively as the way you present yourself. Again, you will need to do your research. Don't be afraid to phone in advance to enquire about the dress code if you are unsure, as in some group interview situations smart casual attire may be required. However, in most cases, professional grooming and attire require following the standards outlined below:

- Overall, clean, neat and tidy appearance.
- A tailored suit in a neutral tone.
- All items of clothing should be clean and pressed.
- Sheer hosiery in a shade that blends with the natural tone of your skin.
- If wearing a skirt, it should be just above or below the knee in length as exposing too much of the thigh area is considered provocative.
- Your aim should be to look professional rather than sexy.
- Wear polished court shoes with the heels clean and in tact.
- Jewelry, embellishments and accessories should not be ostentatious but plain and kept to a minimum.
- Fingernails should be clean and manicured and nail polish should be neutral.
- Hair should be clean, styled appropriately and not appear disheveled.
- If you are required to wear a nametag, it should be fastened to the right side of your most outer garment opposite your heart.

POSITIVE ATTITUDE

People can sense your attitude from afar so it makes sense that one should aim to convey the right one. Always remember that every employer is looking for two things: someone that will be best suited to a specific role, and someone who will cohere with the specific culture of their organization. In order to show that you fit every aspect of this criteria you have to embody a respectful approach in your quest for employment. This is easily achieved by adopting an 'I need them more than they need me' attitude. By being humble, you are directly acknowledging a person's position and status. Remember, while it is important to be confident in your own skin, it is vital to ensure you don't come across as being over-confident. Ensure your body language is sending the right signals as well—do not slouch, yawn, chew gum, stretch or rest your hands behind your head. This type of behavior will be perceived as arrogant and ruin your chances of securing a position of any kind, or worse, contribute to building a bad reputation.

Honesty plays an integral role in a person being perceived by others as sincere. In an interview, if you don't understand a question, or you are feeling nervous, rest assured that this will not hinder your chances of employment if handled correctly. In fact, admitting to being nervous in an interview if you have difficulty answering a question can be endearing. It shows that you are human and that you're making a conscious effort to make a good impression.

WHAT TO SAY IN AN INTERVIEW

There are certain questions that are universal when it comes to being interviewed and you should prepare your answers to these well in advance. This will take away any nervous tension associated with the unknown element of the interview process and allow you to focus on making a good impression. When you are asked about your interests, the employer is looking for information that may indicate what sort of person you are. For example, if you were being interviewed as a sales clerk in a bookshop and you didn't mention when asked that you enjoy reading, it would be highly likely that you would not be deemed as the right person for the position. Similarly, answering 'I don't know' to questions about yourself isn't appealing and conveys an air of disinterest and apathy.

At some stage, you will be asked to speak about your strengths and weaknesses. How you answer this question is very important and you should always tailor your response to the qualities you think the employer is looking for. For example, if you will be employed as part of a team, mentioning that you are a team player will serve you well. Similarly, stating that you pride yourself on your communication skills would be an attractive quality in somebody looking to work in sales. Whatever the position may be, do your research, be savvy and be sincere.

When it comes to discussing your weaknesses in an interview, be mindful not to come across arrogant by saying that you don't have any. Rephrase the question in your answer by responding, 'some areas in which I'd like to develop are…'. This willingness to grow professionally gives the impression that you are enthusiastic and that you possess high standards. These are attractive qualities to any employer.

HOW TO RESPOND TO REJECTION

If you aren't successful in your application for whatever reason, it is important to respond to the news appropriately. If you are notified by mail, you don't necessarily need to respond. If you are notified by telephone, however, you should always ask for feedback as it leaves the employer with the impression that you have high standards when it comes to professional development. Asking where you could have improved in the interview process enables you to grow from the experience and refine your interview technique. Ensure you thank the employer for the opportunity and remain polite, even though you may feel more disgruntled than delighted. This will ensure you reinforce the good impression they already have of you from the interview. You never know, according to them, you may be next in line or more suitable for another role. Whatever the case, you want to avoid burning bridges at all times.

PROFESSIONAL ETIQUETTE

"If you have great talents, industry will improve them; if moderate abilities, industry will supply their deficiencies. Nothing is denied to well-directed labor: nothing is ever to be attained without it."
—Sir Joshua Reynolds

Once you have secured a job, you need to make sure you keep it. This involves working to a high standard, adhering to company policy and maintaining a level of professionalism. Being professional means to behave in a manner that is suitable for a work environment and conducive to productivity and performance.

PROFESSIONAL TELEPHONE ETIQUETTE

When speaking on the telephone at work, it is likely that you will be speaking on behalf of, or representing your employer. This means that you have to apply their standards rather than your own. Always answer the phone clearly, stating your name and the name of the business. Remember, your sole purpose is to create a positive impression of your place of work by assisting the caller as much as you can. This leaves the caller feeling positive about their interaction with you and therefore, positive about your employer.

PROFESSIONAL EMAIL ETIQUETTE

Whether you are an employee of a small business or a multinational corporation, your correspondence with colleagues, customers and clients is a direct reflection of the professional standards of your employer. Therefore, any form of professional communication, whether electronic or otherwise, should remain as such. Emails should follow a specific structure beginning with a salutation (the most common being 'Dear') followed by the person's name. The body of the email should be written in formal register, avoiding slang, nicknames and personal anecdotes of any kind. Ensure close attention is paid to grammar and punctuation throughout in order to convey a standard of excellence. Sign off with 'Regards,' and include a signature with your full name, your title and/or position and your contact details.

EMAIL DO'S AND DON'TS

- Ensure your email address reflects your professionalism by avoiding pet names such as 'butterflies@happyglittermail.com'.
- Never send an email when you're upset or angry. You are likely to write something you will later regret. Wait until the next day when you have calmed down.
- Never use the 'Bcc:' feature (blind carbon copy) field to spy on people. Use it to keep certain email addresses confidential.
- Avoid the use of sarcasm and personal jokes in any email correspondence.
- Be clear and make your point quickly.

- Never send any email you wouldn't want displayed in the office lunchroom. You have no control over where your email will go once you have sent it.
- Do not send emails of cute animals doing cute things or any other such chain mail to your colleagues. Always assume that people are too busy to read junk mail.
- Never press 'Reply All' unless absolutely necessary for the same reason.
- Edit your email before you fill in the 'To:' field.
- DO NOT TYPE IN CAPS UNLESS YOU MEAN TO INDICATE SHOUTING!

IN THE OFFICE

Working in an office with other people can be a wonderful opportunity to develop interpersonal and communication skills, learn about being a part of a team and strengthen morale. Professional development aside, working in an office can also be an opportunity to make life-long friends and associates. However, given the close proximity to others, it is essential that basic principles of etiquette are applied to ensure a safe, comfortable and productive working environment for all.

BATHROOM ETIQUETTE

- Never take any reading material into the bathroom with you.
- Always lock the cubicle door once inside for your privacy and the comfort of others.
- Clean up after yourself. If you need to use the toilet brush, do so.

- If air freshener is available, use it.
- Flush the toilet after every use.
- Be considerate of others' privacy; avoid congregating in the bathroom to have conversations.
- Wash your hands thoroughly with soap and water in order to prevent the spread of germs.
- If you use the last piece of toilet paper, replace it.

KITCHEN ETIQUETTE

- Always clean up after yourself by placing everything you use back in its place. This includes cleaning surfaces on which you have left remnants of food.
- After using a sponge, ensure it is clean and ready for use by the next person. Wash and wring out the sponge and place it by the sink.
- Never eat food or use condiments that do not belong to you.
- Make an effort to discard any foodstuffs belonging to you that may have passed their use by date.
- If preparing food in a communal microwave oven or sandwich toaster, ensure you wipe them down afterward.

"When I got here… they thought I worked 100 hours a day. Now, no matter what time I get in, nobody questions my ability to get the job done. Get it through your head, first impressions last. You start behind the eight ball, you'll never get in front."
—*Harvey Specter*

PROFESSIONAL DO'S AND DON'TS

- Be punctual every day, the earlier, the better.
- Be polite and considerate of others around you.
- Avoid gossip. Gossiping about the personal affairs of others is rude and won't benefit you at all. It may even earn you a bad reputation.
- Always treat headphones as the 'do not disturb' sign of the workplace. When worn by co-workers, it is likely a conscious decision on their part to tune out and get to work.
- Be mindful of the things you say. Workplaces are full of people from all walks of life so you need to be sure you aren't going to offend anybody by making flippant remarks. Do not make comments or jokes that may be interpreted as offensive by anybody else, regardless of whether or not you mean anything by them. This includes but is not limited to comments made about race, religion, ethnicity, sexual inclination, gender, hairstyle, weight etc.
- Treat others with respect and dignity no matter what their position in the social hierarchy.
- Greet your co-workers when you arrive and say goodbye when you leave. This is common courtesy and reflects a positive attitude.
- Always remain in control of your emotions at work. Do not shout, swear or do anything that may be perceived as throwing a tantrum. Keep cool and calm so that you can be better equipped to make better choices.
- Avoid slang. The language you use at work should have a professional tone.

- Be mindful of others by behaving in a manner that doesn't hinder their productivity in any way. This includes being constantly chatty or disruptive.
- Separate your personal life from your professional one. Unless you are on a break, never make personal calls or use social media when you are being paid to get a particular job done.
- At work functions of any kind, approach any consumption of alcohol with caution in order to avoid intoxication. Remaining in control of your behavior in any professional setting is imperative if you wish to be taken seriously.

> *"You cannot dream yourself into a character;*
> *you must hammer and forge yourself one."*
> —Henry David Thoreau

WORK FUNCTIONS AND CHRISTMAS PARTY ETIQUETTE

Annual office Christmas parties can be a lot of fun. They allow you to mingle with co-workers on a social level, strengthen existing professional relationships and create new ones. You mustn't be fooled, however, despite the bells and whistles, glitz and glam, a social work function is still just that and one wrong move could spell disaster for any budding career. You need to be mindful of the way you are projecting your professional image—stay on brand. The way you behave is an outward projection of who you are, so do kick your heels up, just be careful not to kick yourself in the process. The following guidelines will help you navigate the most treacherous of work functions:

- Never binge drink or become intoxicated. This is the fastest way to ruin a reputation. Maintaining control over your faculties is essential in any professional context.
- Avoid excessive flattery, especially toward those people who you perceive to be in positions of power. This can cause awkwardness and may make you appear insincere.
- Never be the last to leave. If anything scandalous occurs, you will be associated with that scandal, whether you were there or not.
- Do not make sexual advances at any of your colleagues, you will be the talk of the office well into the future.
- Avoid dressing too provocatively, your professional image could bear the brunt of the backlash.
- Mingle. Don't be afraid to converse with people that aren't in your immediate circle of friends and use these conversations as networking opportunities.
- Do not engage in any illegal behavior including the consumption of illegal drugs. Not only would you be breaking the law but you would risk causing irreparable damage to any future career prospects.

CUSTOMER SERVICE

"A customer is the most important visitor on our premises. He is not dependent on us. We are dependent on him. He is not an interruption on our work. He is the purpose of it. He is not an outsider on our business. He is a part of it. We are not doing him a favor by serving him. He is doing us a favor by giving us an opportunity to do so."
—*Kenneth B. Elliott*

Customer service isn't merely about accepting payment from people, it's about creating a positive experience. Made up of a complex set of skills, customer service requires training, knowledge and foresight. It demands the most proficient of people skills, the most pronounced problem solving ability and a willingness to go above and beyond for the satisfaction of the customer. If you are employed in the service industry, or wish to be, there are various qualities you need to embody in order to be successful.

Impeccable customer service skills cannot exist in the absence of a positive attitude. Demonstrating outwardly attractive behavior is the first step toward customer satisfaction. You are an extension of the business you represent, so your attitude sends a very clear signal about the quality of the product or service that is being provided by that business.

Product knowledge is essential in building trust with potential customers. You need to be informed and possess a thorough understanding of the product or service you are selling so you can adequately cater to the customer's needs. Never try to feign knowledge, if you are asked a question and you don't know the answer, be honest and do your utmost to find it. This demonstrates your willingness to assist.

Be patient. Sometimes people aren't exactly sure what they want. Regardless, never rush a customer into making a decision and avoid becoming frustrated at all costs. As soon as you become tense, the customer can only assume that you are annoyed by their indecision. Behave as though their indecision is a pleasure and reassure them if they apologize. In cases such as these it is up to you to read between the lines. This is where the skill of being perceptive is beneficial. Try to ask probing questions that give you a good idea of the type of product or service they may be looking for.

Sometimes and without warning, frustrated or disgruntled customers may take their displeasure out on you. If this happens, keeping your cool is of utmost importance. Diffusing irrational behavior is another valuable skill worth mastering. Quite simply, the louder a person becomes, the quieter you become.

The more emotional a person becomes, the more logical your approach. Always insist that you will do all that is in your power to remedy the situation and approach solving the problem with a sense of urgency. Never hesitate to seek the expert opinion of a supervisor or manager; this will be perceived as initiative, which is an attractive quality to any employer.

CUSTOMER SERVICE DO'S AND DON'TS

- Smiling is the best indication of positivity so smile, stand tall and ensure you are impeccably presented.
- Demonstrate perfect manners.
- Greet your customers warmly and ask if they need assistance. If they decline, let them know you are willing to assist if they change their mind.
- Be sure to demonstrate open body language.
- Never slouch or lean on any surfaces as this indicates boredom or lethargy. You want to avoid looking anything but enthusiastic.
- Do not chew gum. If you are conscious of oral hygiene, use breath mints as an alternative.
- Engage in productive behavior when you have no customers or clients. Ensure glass surfaces are clean and polished, that stock is available and that displays of merchandise are in order etc.
- Be approachable. Do not make or receive personal calls, or have friends come in to socialize with you. This may detract potential customers.
- Ensure your professional communications such as telephone and email correspondence are of the highest standard. (See: Chapter 4)
- Listen to what the customer is saying. What do they need? Try to identify this and make suggestions based on the information they are giving you.
- If you have a disgruntled customer, approach rudeness with

kindness and emotions with logic. Ask them if you can fix the problem, and if you can't, the possible options known to them. If the customer wishes to lodge a formal complaint, offer the necessary information graciously and apologize for any inconvenience.

RESIGNATION ETIQUETTE

Deciding to leave your place of work for whatever reason, should never have a negative impact on the progression of your future career. For the process of transition to run as smoothly as possible, consideration needs to be taken when dealing with your co-workers and your employer. In order for this to occur, certain rules need to be adhered to.

–   Always have another job before leaving one. Most employers look for gaps in resumes as a means of filtering through potential interview candidates. If your resume says that you are currently employed, this will work in your favor when seeking out other employment.

–   Alert your employer to the fact that you are resigning before you tell your co-workers. Do this by writing a letter. A letter of resignation should be professional in tone, clear and to the point. Avoid listing personal reasons for your decision, it is much better to include a statement of thanks for the experience you have gained while working there.

–   Give notice. Usually two weeks is an acceptable time frame, provided you are not bound to a contractual agreement which states otherwise.

- Do not speak negatively about your place of work or express feelings of ill will to do with any part of your decision to leave. Even if your anger is justified, never show it. Leaving a place of employment on a bad note can be detrimental to your reputation.
- Ensure you take the time to clean up any files you may have, either in a cabinet or on a computer. You wouldn't want others looking through files that may be confidential in nature or no longer relevant.
- Take all your personal belongings with you and clean your working area, be it a desk or otherwise, to a standard acceptable for another person to begin work upon. Your replacement should not have to clean their work-station before they start work.
- Personally say farewell to people and warmly thank anybody that may have helped you along the way. If a speech is made on behalf of your co-workers in acknowledgement of your efforts, it is polite to respond accordingly. This speech need not be a long one, but all the same, do prepare a few words ahead of time if you feel anxious or nervous about it.
- Do ask for a written reference from your employer. Regardless of whether your new job is similar or you are changing industries completely, a written reference will add to your resume and serve as a testament to your character.

GROOMING AND PRESENTATION

"The height of sophistication is simplicity."
—*Clare Boothe Luce*

It's no secret that the cliché 'Don't judge a book by its cover' came about as a result of our eagerness to make assumptions based on appearance. As it happens, we haven't taken our own advice and continue to judge people and things accordingly. Although initially that statement sounds shallow, let's think of our presentation as an extension of good manners.

People make assumptions about one another based on first impressions, so knowing how to dress appropriately for certain occasions is very important if you want people to take you seriously. The way we dress speaks volumes about our attitude and conveys an air of self-respect. Most organizations will have a professional dress code or uniform policy that requires strict adherence. Be mindful that in order to benefit from the good reputation of an organization that you are a part of, you need to be proactive in maintaining its standards.

DRESS CODES EXPLAINED

Casual. To dress casually means that you should dress for comfort. This will vary according to individual taste and culture. Generally speaking, denim jeans and T-shirts are considered casual, as is beachwear, active or leisurewear is also acceptable. Dressing casually is never appropriate in the workplace it should be worn only when comfort takes priority over presentation.

Smart Casual. The refined version of casual, this dress code has various interpretations depending on the social setting. As a general rule, smart casual refers to looking neat and tidy and is considered a step up from casual dressing. Avoid active wear or beachwear if smart casual dress is required. Also, if wearing denim, ensure it is combined with a dressier piece to give a more polished look. Smart casual may also refer to clothing more suited to garden parties and tea parties, in which case, dresses may also be considered smart-casual.

Professional. Professional dress is neat, tidy, conservative and polished. It is a standard of dress that conveys an attitude of excellence. If your personal presentation reflects attention to detail, others will assume you apply those same standards to your work. Similarly, if your appearance demonstrates a lack of care and attention, it's safe to assume that your work ethic will be judged in the same way. Go for a tailored well-put-together aesthetic rather than a provocative one. If you want your bosses, mentors and colleagues to take you seriously and respect your work, you need them to consider you an asset before they consider your assets.

Semi-Formal/Cocktail. If an invitation states that the dress code is semi-formal or cocktail, a short to three-quarter length dress is appropriate, so too are stylish separates. Semi-formal dressing came about at a time when it was fashionable to serve pre-dinner drinks such as cocktails before a more formal meal. It is the level of dress above smart casual and beneath the formal black tie dress code. If unsure, select fabrics that would be considered dressier than those fabrics more suitable for casual clothing. Silk for example, would be more suitable than loosely woven cotton for this dress code. Always opt for stylish elegance.

Formal/Black Tie. The clothing required at functions with this dress code is a long, formal dinner dress or gown, depending on the event. If you have been invited to a black tie dinner for instance, a three-quarter-length cocktail dress may be suitable. If however the event happens to be a ball or other such occasion, a gown is more appropriate. It is not customary for gloves to be worn unless royalty are present.

White Tie. This type of dress is reserved for balls at which royalty are present. Long gowns and long white gloves are appropriate, as is elaborate jewelry and in some cases, a tiara. Traditionally, gowns with wide skirts were worn for dancing and strapless dresses were allowed for the display of extravagant jewelry.

GROOMING

In the same way that taking care of ourselves is good for our physical and mental health, personal grooming and hygiene are equally important when it comes to first impressions. Being clean, neat and tidy sends a clear message that you respect yourself, as well as others around you. Try to incorporate the following into your daily routine:

- Always ensure you bathe and use soap at least once a day.
- Apply antiperspirant deodorant to your underarms after bathing.
- Ensure your fingernails and toenails are clean and manicured.
- Wash your hair with shampoo as often as you see fit but no less than three times per week. It should be brushed and styled appropriately.
- Shave your legs if appropriate.

SARTORIAL DO'S AND DON'TS

- Wear clothes that suit your body shape.
- Dress for the weather.
- Always look clean and tidy.
- Ensure items of clothing are clean and pressed.
- If provided, always adhere to the dress code.
- Dress for the job you want rather than the job you have.
- Take pride in your appearance, it conveys an air of self-respect.
- Aim to look professional rather than provocative in a professional setting.
- Ensure your shoes are polished and re-heel when necessary.

- Dress appropriately for your age.
- Avoid exposing your cleavage when wearing a miniskirt or dress. As a general rule, select one or the other. Think mystique not mistake.
- Never wear hosiery with open toe shoes. Hosiery is designed to give the appearance of perfect skin, so exposing your stocking-covered toes would ruin the illusion.

FRAGRANCE

While wearing fragrance can uplift the senses and add the finishing touch to any outfit, the type of fragrance worn needs to be given some consideration. Use the following rules as a guide:
- Fragrances vary according to the concentration of essential oils within them. Eau de toilette is the least concentrated, eau de parfum increases in intensity and parfum is the strongest. Bear this in mind when applying your fragrance and remember the golden rule: less is more.
- Your fragrance should only be noticeable to people who are standing no more than an arms' distance away from you. If your fragrance enters a room before you do, you are wearing far too much. When applying fragrance with a spray, two sprays, one on the inside of each wrist, are ample. Be sure to spray from a distance so as not to cause pool of liquid that may drip onto clothing. Due to its concentration, parfum will come in a smaller bottle without a spray. When using it, remember that a tiny dab of fragrance on the pulse points of the wrist or the neck is sufficient.

- Never use fragrance to mask the fact that you haven't bathed. Fragrance should always be applied to clean skin.
- Adapt your fragrance style to suit your environment. For example, if you are going to work, select a subtle fragrance that is fresh and light rather than bold and heady. It is important to be considerate of those that work closest to you. Similarly, strong, musky fragrances that pack an olfactory punch are more suitable for night time and should be worn sparingly.

HATS

Hats come in and out of fashion like the tide. Whether in vogue or not, the only time a lady is required to remove her fashion hat is if it is obstructing the view of others. If wearing a baseball-style cap, however, the same rules apply to both ladies and gentlemen. Removing one's hat is a sign of respect and always appropriate inside homes, at mealtimes, in restaurants and cafes, while being introduced, inside places of worship (unless a head covering is required) and whenever a national anthem is played. Unless they are part of a uniform or safety requirement, hats should not be worn inside where professional dress standards apply.

SKINCARE AND MAKEUP

"For beautiful eyes, look for the good in others; for beautiful lips, speak only words of kindness; and for poise, walk with the knowledge you are never alone."
—Sam Levenson

We all know that makeup can do wonders for a girl's face. It can make your skin look like butterscotch, your eyes look like butterflies and your lips look like shiny toffee apples. Considering that most people have a sweet tooth, makeup can be a girl's best friend. There's makeup for your skin that can make you look like you just returned from a two week holiday by the beach, cream that makes your skin sparkle like the seashore and treatments and potions to transform your hair from fried straw to soft, luscious locks. For that finishing touch, there are fragrances that can get you smelling like a candy store, a florist, a summer's day, freshly baked cookies or a coconut. Unfortunately though, makeup can also be your foe. For example, drawing thick, black circles around your lash line does not enhance beauty; it looks stupid. Eyeliner is for making your lashes look thicker, not for turning you into a panda—pandas are cute in the wild, not on your face.

There's a fine line between getting foundation right and creating a disaster. Getting foundation wrong can make even a few pimples look like small animals are trying to burrow their way out of your face or worse, like you fell asleep in your porridge. The secret to makeup success is making it look natural. This doesn't mean wear less (some girls feel more comfortable with a little extra help), just try to work with what you have and follow the steps below.

1. The most important step in the process is getting your skin looking and feeling healthy, smooth and hydrated. Find a cleanser that suits your skin type and your budget and use it daily.

2. Even if you have oily skin, you need to moisturize your face after every wash. If your skin feels rough or patchy after cleansing, use a gentle exfoliant afterward (a damp face-cloth will do if you don't have anything suitable for the sensitive skin on your face).

3. Now that your skin is silky smooth, you need to even out the tone. If your skin is even all over, skip this step and giggle with glee as you gaze at your perfect skin in the mirror. For those girls that aren't so lucky, start off by matching your foundation to the exact tone of your skin. This way, you'll avoid that horrid mask-line around your jaw and you'll be able to create a good base for the rest.

4. Lightly brush on some bronzer so that you don't look like a shiny alien. Usually, the fatter the brush, the better the finish when it comes to powders and bronzers. There are a few rules you must never break when it comes to bronzer: never apply so much that your face and neck are different tones. Always continue the bronzer down to your neck and remember to blend through to your hairline and ears. If you have fair skin, always choose honey tones rather than orange ones and keep trying until you find one that suits you.

5. Next stop, eyes. People often refer to eyes as being 'windows to the soul'. Sometimes though, when a makeup disaster strikes, potentially beautiful eyes can look more like the remnants of two rogue parrots that crash-landed on your face. To stop this from happening, use natural hues. Experiment with shades of beige and brown and blend with your finger or a brush until there is no obvious line. Lightly pencil over your top and bottom lash lines with eyeliner and apply two coats of mascara. If you're beginning to panic, don't worry. Eyeliner doesn't suit everybody and you can skip this step completely and still look amazing.

LIPSTICK ETIQUETTE

Whether you prefer a matte or glossy finish, the trick to a perfect pout is to use different shades of nudes and pinks to enhance the natural shade of your lips. Gloss makes the lip appear fuller while dark shades tend to do the opposite. Experiment with bright lipstick when the social calendar calls and for anything else, aim for a natural look.

Reapply lipstick in the bathroom rather than in public. Remember that the purpose of makeup is to enhance your natural features— you wouldn't want others to think that you painted your face on; it would ruin the illusion of effortless beauty.

When dining, always wipe your lips on a tissue before using a cloth napkin so that you don't make a mess. You should avoid inconveniencing the host at all costs.

CHAPTER 6

SOCIAL GRACES

"Circumspection in calamity; mercy in greatness; good speeches
in assemblies; fortitude in adversity: these are the self-attained
perfections of great souls."
—Hitopadesha

PUTTING OTHERS AT EASE

People respond positively to those that demonstrate attractive behavior. By being considerate of others and making people feel comfortable, you will be considered polite by those you meet. Every aspect of manners and etiquette, every polite gesture, it all comes down to this simple philosophy: Wherever you are, whatever the social setting, putting other's needs before your own is the easiest way to ensure you are being perceived by others as well mannered.

TELEPHONE ETIQUETTE

The humble telephone's metamorphosis into a high-speed internet connecting, picture taking, call making, social media publishing, photo editing, music playing, information downloading device, has made the world seem significantly smaller. While the possibilities of access to the world online are boundless, there are still times when the use of a personal electronic device is inappropriate, especially in the company of others.

For many, being on the phone has become second nature. The use of smartphones to alleviate boredom and to escape from the awkwardness of unfamiliar social situations has become commonplace. However, as we immerse ourselves further and further into the realm of our lives that exists online, we begin to lose touch with real people and with reality. If you wish to be perceived as somebody who is well mannered and confident, you need to give the impression that you are present and willing to participate, even if only in a conversation. Ultimately, in social situations we must be careful not to convey the message that we would rather be elsewhere, doing other things. It is just plain rude.

SMARTPHONE USE DO'S AND DON'TS

- Never place your phone on the dinner table. The suggestion that it may take priority if necessary is discourteous to the people with whom you are sharing a meal.
- Don't call, answer, text or anything else while engaging or interacting with other people. This includes listening to somebody speak, whether you are interested in what they say is irrelevant.
- If you need to answer an urgent call (something in need of your immediate attention) simply excuse yourself and walk away so as not to interrupt or distract others.
- Respect others' right to privacy by avoiding using the speaker function on your phone unless you are in a private setting.

- Turn your phone off or switch it to silent mode if you are part of an audience, a group or in a professional environment. It is polite to consider others' right to a quiet place.
- Avoid speaking loudly on your phone on public transport, in waiting rooms and in queues in general. Just as it is considered rude to eavesdrop or listen in on others' conversations, so too is it rude to force your conversations upon them.
- Avoid using your phone in your daily interactions with others. Give the people with whom you are interacting with your full attention. This conveys a sense of respect for the person and/or the service that is being provided to you.

THE ART OF CONVERSATION

"The Art of Conversation: A certain self-control
which now holds the subject, now lets it go with
a respect for the emergencies of the moment."
—Ralph Waldo Emerson

Making conversation can be intimidating at the best of times, let alone with somebody you have never met. The important thing to note here is that if you make a person feel at ease in your company, conversation will flow naturally, without hesitation or awkwardness. Think of face-to-face conversation as the real-life version of looking at somebody's social media profile, it's a mutual download of information that may serve as a gateway to learning, employment or even a lasting friendship—the opportunities are endless.

There are guidelines that you can follow that once mastered, will give you the confidence you need to make the right impression on whoever you choose.

First of all, you need to know how to introduce yourself properly (see: Chapter 2—Introductions). The next step is to assess what you wish to achieve from the conversation. If unsure, your purpose should simply be to create a good impression. Then, once the first step is complete, you need to go about the mutual download of information in a manner that causes the least offence to the other person. Remember, if you are attempting to make someone feel at ease in your company, it is quite difficult to cause offence.

MASTERING THE ART OF CONVERSATION

− Avoid asking personal questions as this may cause a person to feel awkward or uncomfortable. Remember, what people deem to be of a personal nature, will vary significantly. Refrain from asking how much a person earns at all times.
− Don't interrupt others while they are speaking.
− Listen attentively and make gestures that subtly communicate your interest such as nodding and smiling.
− Do not speak about yourself excessively or brag about your achievements. Think of a conversation as a two-way street, you mustn't try to run anyone off the road.
− Be pleasant and polite.
− If in a group, do not exclude anybody from the conversation by focusing on one particular person.
− Make an effort to make eye contact with those with whom you are speaking.

- Avoid controversial topics that are likely to arouse emotive responses, such as religion or politics. People have wide ranging views and in a social setting, you should avoid any subjects that are likely to cause conflict.
- Adapt your level of language to suit the person with whom you are speaking. For example, if speaking to an acquaintance at a party, what you say and how you say it would differ considerably to the way you would speak to your boss at a work function.

TO SPEAK OR NOT TO SPEAK

Knowing when it is appropriate to speak is vital when it comes to making a good impression and ensuring others remain at ease in your company. What you say and do not say contributes to others perceptions of you in more ways than one. Ultimately, it's about understanding the messages you are sending out and learning to be in control of them. As a general guide, ensure you take note of the following rules:

- Don't interrupt others while they are speaking, it is discourteous.
- Respect others' right to listen by resisting the urge to comment or chat at a presentation or meeting, during a speech, at the theater, cinema or during a performance.
- Don't invite yourself into other people's conversations. If someone is interested in your opinion, they will ask for it.
- If you are asked a question to which you don't know the answer, say you don't know rather than attempting to fumble

your way through a contrived response. This will make you appear insincere and disingenuous.

– Have the confidence not to respond to awkward, personal or inappropriate questions by politely declining to comment.

ACCEPTING AN AWARD

Awards are an important way to show appreciation and acknowledge individual achievement and success in society. Whether the setting is educational, professional, formal or informal, it is polite to acknowledge the gesture by thanking those responsible. When accepting an award it is imperative that you respond in the proper manner.

In a formal awards ceremony, recipients will be notified in advance. An acceptance speech may be required so take the time to prepare a few words of thanks. This shows that you are grateful to have been selected and motivates others to strive for excellence, which ultimately, is the overarching purpose of any awards ceremony. Recipients should accept awards with the left hand while using the right to shake hands (see: Chapter 2—The Handshake). It is also important to dress accordingly. If unsure, enquire about the dress code and ensure your clothes are clean and pressed. In some cases you may be required to respond with a verbal acknowledgement of the award. If so, it is considered proper etiquette to thank the founder of the award and everybody involved in the selection process. In addition, to comment on the benefits of being involved in such a process ensures you are seen as a person who values effort, achievement and excellence.

In an informal setting with a smaller audience such as a meeting of employees in a workplace, less emphasis should be placed on acceptance speeches due to the impromptu nature of the awards. However, it is imperative that you express your gratitude upon receipt of the award by initiating a handshake, as well as verbally expressing your thanks.

AWARD ACCEPTANCE DO'S AND DON'TS

- Dress accordingly and don't be afraid to enquire about the dress code in advance. If there is no dress code, ensure your attire is clean and pressed and that your hair is neat and tidy.
- Arrive 15 minutes early in case of any changes in the order of events.
- Shake the hand of the person who gives you the award, make eye contact and say thank you.
- If required to stand for a certain amount of time either alone or with other award recipients, ensure you stand up straight, and look ahead.
- Avoid fidgeting, looking down and chewing gum.
- After the audience applause (never applaud yourself), return to your allocated seat.

MAKING A SPEECH

The mere thought of speaking in front of a crowd is daunting for many, yet something that most people will experience at some stage in their lives. Regardless of age or experience, anxiety levels can reach dizzying heights, with sweaty palms, redness and trembling limbs all working together to sabotage our attempts to appear in control. However, there is a certain set of rules that can be followed to ensure public speaking success.

First of all, there are certain things you can do to reduce nervous tension immediately. If you have access to a lectern, use it to hold your notes and to rest your hands while you speak. Having something to hold on to disguises any obvious trembling. Next, know your audience and adjust the level of your language accordingly. For instance, when speaking in a formal context, avoid colloquial expressions and slang. This is very important if you wish to be taken seriously. Your aim should be to be understood, so clarity is of utmost importance.

Secondly, know your material by heart. If you have a thorough understanding of the information you are presenting, it is a lot easier to focus on the conventions of public speaking such as voice projection, eye contact, pace, gesture and tone. To project your voice means to be heard by your audience without having to scream or shout at them. This skill is relatively simple to master with a little practice. If using a microphone, adjust it to suit your height rather than bending down toward it. While speaking, it is important to ensure that you are intermittently making eye contact with the members of your audience. This gives you credibility and ensures you are perceived as sincere. As you speak, be mindful of your pace. Speaking quickly, increases your anxiety by making breathing difficult. Ensure your speech is easy to follow by taking breaths where appropriate. Don't be afraid to use your hands when speaking, as gestures help place emphasis on important pieces of information.

Lastly, try to vary the tone of your voice so as to avoid sounding robotic. Keeping the audience's attention is vital and speaking in monotone is the fastest way to ensure they tune out.

PUBLIC SPEAKING DO'S AND DON'TS

- Know your audience.
- Know your material.
- Focus on three central points to keep the audiences' attention.
- Ensure you utilize the conventions of speech giving: voice
- Projection, eye contact, gesture, pace and tone.
- Match the level of your speech to your audience and the occasion.
- Avoid use of the word 'um', slang and any other language that could be deemed as inappropriate.

GIFTS: GIVING AND RECEIVING

Gifts are universal symbols of appreciation and acknowledgement. Whether for birthdays, weddings, anniversaries, graduations, religious ceremonies or as token gestures, giving the perfect gift, when executed correctly, can be one of life's most delightfully simple pleasures. After all, who doesn't like a present?

Many people feel anxious when it comes to selecting appropriate gifts for others and this can happen for a number of reasons. The gifts we choose to give say a lot about our intentions so wishing not to be perceived in a certain way or to cause offence to the recipient can be a significant hindrance to the selection process. Luckily, there are some easy to follow guidelines that may alleviate any unnecessary pressure.

A general rule to go by is that if the event or occasion involves a host going to some amount of effort to have you, then a gift is appropriate. For instance, if you are invited to dinner, you should always take a small gift as a token of your appreciation for the efforts of the host. Chocolates are an excellent choice and, depending on your age, so is a bottle of wine. If you're bound by a strict budget, beautifully presented homemade cookies or other such treats are also a great option, so be as creative as you wish. Flowers on the other hand may cause the host unnecessary stress as it is considered impolite not to put flowers in water immediately. This can be difficult while trying to prepare dinner and attend to other guests as they arrive. When it comes to birthdays, it is customary to select gifts that you think the recipient would like as opposed to something you would like. It really is the thought that counts so you want to reflect that some amount of thought has gone into the selection process, especially if the recipient is a close friend. Whatever your budget, a little effort can go a long way. Remember, gifts of sentimental value are often worth far more than anything with a price tag.

Gift wrapping can be a hellish experience for some, but when done correctly can make the most simple of gifts seem extra special. Paper and ribbon should be of a high quality. This ensures easy folding and a smooth finish. Avoid fancy designs or embellishments such as glitter; the most elegant wrapping is often the plainest. Ensure that tape is not visible from underneath the folds of the paper and if you are dealing with an oddly shaped item, place it inside a box of a similar size before attempting to wrap it.

When receiving a gift from a person, it is polite to say thank you and open it immediately. Commenting on the design and/or quality of the wrapping is also acceptable. However, if a gift is being given to you as the host of a party, you are not obliged to open it immediately. Being a host, you may be too busy preparing to open gifts. If this is the case, show appreciation by putting gifts aside to open later. Avoid setting it down haphazardly and going about your business, this could be interpreted as a blatant disregard for the effort of the person who brought you the gift.

SENDING CARDS

Greeting Cards. Greeting cards are great way to express our well wishes, gratitude and condolences to the people in our lives. In a world where most communication happens instantly, taking the time to write a personal, thoughtful message in a card is indicative of good character. A card should always address the recipient directly and contain a thoughtful message with specific reference to the occasion. The recipient should be addressed by their title and name depending on their relationship to you. For example, a peer can be addressed by their first name only, whereas the parent of a friend would be addressed by their title and surname: 'Dear Mrs. Smith'. Your relationship to the person should always dictate the level of familiarity in the message. Sign off with your full name formally, or informally, as you wish.

Birthday Cards. Birthday cards should include well wishes and be celebratory in tone. If you do not feel comfortable writing a personalized birthday message to someone, choosing a one with a pre-written message inside is perfectly acceptable. There are plenty to choose from, so do take the time to be thoughtful in your selection.

Thank You Cards. These should be sent within a week of receiving a gift and should include a message that expresses your gratitude as well as a comment on how the gift will be used.

Cards of Condolence. To express sympathy and support to a grieving person in acknowledgement of their loss, you should send a card of condolence and offer thoughtful words of encouragement.

APOLOGIES

"In this life, when you deny someone an apology, you will remember it at a time when you beg forgiveness."
—*Toba Beta*

Everybody makes mistakes, some more frequently than others. The ability to apologize for any wrong doing is an important quality to possess. Not only does it strengthen one's character, enabling growth and personal development, it also demonstrates integrity and the desire to restore relationship equilibrium. Learning how to apologize is the first step. It will help you overcome adversity and enable you to move on from various situations that life throws in your direction.

- Always apologize to someone face to face. Never email, text or phone as these methods are far too impersonal.
- When apologizing, be sincere. Never apologize if you do not mean it. The average person can instantly sense a feigned apology so leave your acting skills at home for this one.

- Take responsibility for 100 percent of your actions. Never apologize expecting one in return or with a view to laying a percentage of the blame on another person.
- If someone is attempting to give you a sincere apology, listen thoughtfully. Go out of your way to acknowledge their efforts by thanking them and accepting their apology.
- When apologizing, look the person in the eyes as a sign of your sincerity. Do not cringe or roll your eyes as this will detract from any sincerity you may have had in the first place.

TOASTS

A toast is an offer of well wishes most commonly used to affirm the reason for a celebratory gathering or mark a memorable event. Toasts can be formal or informal. However, it is imperative that you avoid using foul language, telling crude or inappropriate jokes and using slang. Even though it may be an opportunity to bathe in the limelight, always remember that a toast isn't about the person making it. In terms of weddings and other such formal occasions, a toast should always make reference to who or what the gathering has been held in honor of. When giving a toast at a wedding celebration, the bride and groom's future happiness should be the theme, while at a less formal dinner party, the efforts of the host should be acknowledged. If you are asked to propose a toast, there is a specific structure to be aware of.

The Introduction. Firstly, address the guests and outline the purpose of the toast, 'Ladies and Gentlemen, I would like to propose a toast to…' Then ensure the guests have filled their glasses (in a formal setting, this will have been done already) and finally invite the guests to be upstanding.

The Body. Express your positive sentiment in no more than four sentences.

The Conclusion. Finally make a short, simple declaration that your audience can repeat in unison and raise your glass. For example, 'To the bride and groom!'. It is correct etiquette for everybody except the toastee, to take a sip from their glass. The person acknowledged in the toast should refrain from standing and should not sip from their glass until after the guests have, otherwise it would appear as though they were toasting themselves.

TAKING PHOTOGRAPHS

Taking photos has become second nature in an age of readily accessible technology. Capturing moments in our daily lives and sharing them on social media, although wonderful, can become tricky when it comes to breaching others' right to privacy. This also applies online. You need to be mindful that whenever you post a photo online, you are effectively publishing it. This not only makes that image visible in a public place, it also gives others access to the image and the ability to use or redistribute it as they wish. Always ensure you check your privacy settings before publishing photos online (see: Chapter 11—Social Media Etiquette).

When taking pictures with friends, it is likely that anybody who does not wish their photo to be taken will say so and/or move away from the scene about to be captured. Whatever the reason, if they object more than once, always respect a person's right not to be photographed. Demanding to know why and incessantly nagging somebody to have their photo taken almost certainly leads to awkwardness and embarrassment.

Something else to consider is that while taking photos enables us to capture various moments in our lives, doing so also removes us from those moments. Experiencing your life through the lens of a camera for the purpose of sharing your experiences with others on social media, significantly affects your ability to be fully present in the experiences that make up your life. Choose to be present; sometimes the lasting memory of being immersed in an experience can be infinitely more vivid than a photograph of it.

PHOTOGRAPHY DO'S AND DON'TS

- Respect signs that prohibit photography regardless of whether or not you know the reason for the ban. Be aware that in some areas, strict guidelines apply and refusal to comply may result in fines and/or more severe penalties.
- Be aware that not all cultures are as photo centric as you may be.
- Be considerate. Not everybody feels comfortable having their photo taken, nor should they be expected to justify themselves upon declining to be photographed.
- Take photos of scenery and various landmarks or tourist

attractions unless signage states otherwise. If you happen to capture people in the background while taking pictures of an historical monument, for instance, you are well within your rights. However, if a person objects to being photographed and tells you so, it is considered polite to erase it immediately.

- Ask permission if you wish to take a photograph of somebody and if you are taking a close-range scenic photo, it is also appropriate to ask permission of those that may be included in the shot.

- Post your photographs online but be mindful of publishing anything may be used as pictorial evidence against you or that may have a negative impact your reputation (see: Chapter 11—Social Media Etiquette).

- When visiting new places, avoid any confusion or uncertainty by doing your research beforehand. Most tourist attractions will have a policy that clearly states whether or not photography is permissible so check the appropriate website or phone for information in advance.

- If you have been invited to attend a private function such as a dinner party, avoid taking photos completely, especially of the inside of someone's home or dinner table. The host has planned to share an experience with certain people and by taking photos and posting them on social media, you are effectively inviting others into the experience. This can be perceived as being discourteous, considering the effort the host may have gone to. Also, by being on your phone, you are sending a clear signal to the host that you would rather be elsewhere.

- Never post photographs of yourself or others in compromising positions. If you capture a candid shot of a friend that casts a negative light on their character, do not redistribute or share it with anybody else. Doing so may have far reaching consequences for you and/or the person in the picture and you don't want to be responsible for bringing your own or anybody else's character into disrepute.

- Do not take photos at funerals, ever. Your sole purpose at a funeral is to commemorate the life of the departed and to pay your respects to their family members. It is highly inappropriate to take photos at such solemn occasions.
- Do not take pictures inside shops such as department stores. A lot of time and effort goes into creating a pleasant shopping experience for the customer. The prohibition of photography is also one way to make it difficult for competitors to mimic merchandising ideas.

LENDING AND BORROWING

Most of us will need to borrow something of someone else's at various stages in our lives, whether it's a car, some money, a dress or a pen. For this reason alone, we need to be thoughtful when it comes to the requests others make of us. Sometimes, being considerate of others means being generous when others need you to be. However, if for some reason you cannot justify lending something to a friend in need, you are well within your rights to decline. This is completely acceptable and should not be considered rude. If in doubt, think of yourself in the same situation before making a decision

Clothing. When borrowing an item of clothing, regardless of its monetary value, there are a few rules that need to be observed, especially if you value your reputation and your friendship with the person doing the lending. Firstly, it is expected that you will treat the item with care, as though it were your own. This means that if your friend wouldn't mud-wrestle in her white silk skirt, neither should you. Secondly, be sure to clean the item before you return it. Generally, depending on the fabric, having clothing dry-cleaned would be appropriate. If you have borrowed an item of clothing and it just isn't right, for any reason, do not take it upon yourself to alter it in any way, ever. It is not yours to alter. Step. Away. From. The. Scissors.

Shoes. Having the same sized feet as a friend with an enviable collection of shoes can be a blessing in times of desperate need. However, if she happens to be generous of heart and you wish to keep the gates of heaven open, you must treat the shoes with the utmost respect. Don't walk through mud, puddles or sand. Stay out of parks and gardens, get off the gravel and steer completely clear of cobblestones. If you are responsible for scuffing or any other damage, take the shoes to be repaired without hesitation. If the damage is irreparable, remember that it is always the responsibility of the borrower to pay for and arrange a replacement.

Cars. If someone graciously lends you their car or any other mode of transport, it is likely that they trust you. If this is the case, you should aim to keep your reputation in tact by being cautious and vigilant about its safe and prompt return. Upon returning it, regardless of the distance traveled, fill the car with petrol to the level indicated by the fuel gauge when you borrowed it. If you drive through a dusty area, or any such conditions which have left the car's surface any less than sparking, do have it cleaned before returning it out of respect for the generosity of the lender.

Luggage. Good quality luggage is very expensive, whether it looks like a briefcase from a technologically advanced parallel universe or a rustically sturdy duffle bag. Be mindful of the fact that in transit, you may not have any control over what happens to the luggage or how it is handled. Either way, its surface is bound to be given a pummeling so be sure to return it in a suitable condition.

LENDING AND BORROWING DO'S AND DON'TS

- Ask nicely and say 'please'.
- Respect the person's right to decline your request.
- Do not beg or make the person feel guilty about their decision.
- Do not ask more than once.
- Never ask a person to justify their decision.
- Never lie about the circumstances surrounding your need to borrow an item.
- Return the item promptly and in the same condition as when you borrowed it.
- Do inform the lender as soon as possible should you damage the item you borrowed.
- Do offer to pay for its replacement or repair.

OUT AND ABOUT

"Do your little bit of good where you are; it's those little bits of good
put together that overwhelm the world."
—Desmond Tutu

QUEUING ETIQUETTE

Whether in a store or at the post office, the bank or the bus stop,
waiting in line is an inevitable part of life. Because of your close
proximity to others, being aware of your personal space at all times
is a must. So, in order to make the experience as comfortable as
possible for all involved, avoid the following: pushing in ahead of
anybody else, staring at people for prolonged periods of time and
encroaching on the personal space of people either side of you.

CINEMA ETIQUETTE

A trip to the movies with friends can be great provided that the
experience isn't ruined by someone else's complete disregard for
cinema etiquette. For any communal activity to work, it is up to the
individuals within that community (in this case, the community
of cinema-goers) to fulfill their side of the bargain, namely, to be

considerate of others. Firstly, everyone that has purchased a ticket should be entitled to equal enjoyment of the film. For this to occur, people need to be mindful of the noise they are making engaging in such things as unwrapping packaged cinema snacks, slurping soda and crunching on popcorn. While most people enjoy a mid-movie snack, keep your personal noises to an absolute minimum. Also, avoid commenting, speaking, or anything that may sabotage others' experience. This includes the use of mobile phones, which should be switched off immediately on entry. Even the backlight of a phone can be a distraction in a dark cinema. Also, avoid resting your feet on the seat, most people don't want their faces near their own feet let alone somebody else's. You may wish to spare a thought to the people employed to clean the cinema too, having to vacuum the tops of the seats in addition to the floor would be time consuming to say the least.

AUDIENCE ETIQUETTE

Being part of an audience, irrespective of its size, is a common occurrence in daily life. Whether an informal gathering, an impromptu meeting or a formal presentation ceremony, the proper conduct of an audience member is of utmost importance. The following rules always apply:
- Be attentive. Avoid slouching, falling asleep.
- Be considerate of others' personal space.
- Do not make noise. Laughter in direct response to intended comedy is acceptable, as is applause. If in doubt, refrain from doing either.

- Never boo or make any sort of outburst, ever.
- Avoid eating unless refreshments are provided.
- Dress appropriately. If unsure, enquire prior to the event.

SPECTATOR ETIQUETTE

Being a spectator at a sporting event can be a lot of fun. While the rules here seem somewhat more relaxed when compared with audience etiquette at the theater, proper conduct is still important for the comfort and safety of all who attend.

- By all means cheer for your team but make sure you are aware of the rules and that you know what you are cheering for.
- Be mindful of your language. Swearing, cursing or any other kind of offensive language is unacceptable. If you are offended by someone's language it would be appropriate to politely ask them to refrain from swearing provided you were not putting yourself in danger by doing so.
- Maintain your dignity by remaining seated when eating or drinking. Depending on the sport, crowds have a tendency to become boisterous and the slightest bump could send food and drink flying into the air, or worse, over other spectators.
- Avoid booing. It does not demonstrate good sportsmanship.

BEACH ETIQUETTE

A day at the beach with family and friends, whether a regular ritual or relaxing trip away can be restorative and renewing for the soul. As with any communal area, it is important you remain aware of the way your actions impact upon the experience of others. At the beach, being attentive of the people around you is essential in getting the most out of the experience. To ensure a great time is had by all, be aware of the following guidelines:

Proximity. Never position yourself beside someone else on the beach unless it is crowded and there are no other spaces available. This is inconsiderate and shows complete disregard for the privacy of other people. If the beach is big, spread out. In such cases where the water is only suitable for swimming in certain areas, sitting next to others is fine. Use your judgment, in crowded areas the acceptable distance between people will have already been established so follow the lead of others.

Sand. Avoid intentionally flicking sand on anybody and be considerate when shaking it off beach towels and items of clothing. Not only will it adhere to any form of moisture, it can make the application of sunscreen virtually impossible! Don't be fooled by the softness of the lovely sand under foot, even the smallest grain of sand in your eye can be agonizing and difficult to remove. If you are responsible for getting sand in the eye of another, apologize profusely and help guide them to the nearest source of fresh water so they may attempt to rinse it out. In any case, prevention is better than cure so be vigilant wherever sand is involved.

Noise. Noise pollution at the beach is commonplace and can be quite annoying for those trying to relax. If you wish to play music, be sure to adjust the volume so that the people closest to you cannot hear it. It would be rude to force your tastes, be they music or otherwise, upon anybody. Also, try not to scream and shout on crowded beaches and keep your conversations at a minimum volume. Nobody should be able to hear the details of your personal anecdotes and nor should you wish them to. Again, this is about being considerate of others so that a good time can be had by all. If playing group games on the beach, by all means do so but find a more secluded area that is further away from those who may be reclining by the shore.

Smoking. Do not smoke at the beach. The breeze will inevitably carry the smoke straight into the nostrils of other beach-goers who should not have to be subjected to the hazardous fumes of others. In addition, cigarette butts pollute the environment and are hazardous to fish, birds and other animals which may mistake them for food.

Seagulls. Do not feed seagulls, ever. Once a seagull has established that there is a plentiful supply of food, every other seagull in the vicinity will make its way toward you. This can be highly annoying for anybody close by trying to relax or eat. A flock of seagulls can be relentless in pursuit of food so always adopt a no tolerance policy.

Litter. When visiting the beach, do not leave litter or food scraps behind, perishable or otherwise. Not only is littering considered an offense, showing complete disregard for the environment is uncouth. As with any goal, its accomplishment lies in the individual's desire to achieve it. We need to be aware of the impact our actions have on the environment and act accordingly if we wish to continue to enjoy the beauty of the natural environment.

THEATER ETIQUETTE

The way we conduct ourselves in a theater not only affects the quality of the performance but the quality of the experience had by all who are present. Therefore, we should convey an air of respect for the performers as well as other members of the audience at all times.

- Arrive early to avoid crowds and to allow for appropriate seating allocation.
- Do not bring your own food or drinks to the theater. You may purchase refreshments from the bar during intermission. If you have something small such as sweets, make sure you do not go about noisily unwrapping them during a performance.
- Phone calls, texting, tweeting, taking photographs and any other such use of a phone is not acceptable in a theater. The backlight of a phone may be visible from the stage so it is important that phones are turned off completely rather than switched to silent mode for sneaky text messaging.
- Do not walk up and down the aisles or leave at any time other than during the intermission.
- Be quiet. Any talking or chatter can be highly distracting and ruin the performance for others.
- Never sing along, regardless of how familiar you are with the music being played. The people beside you are there to hear the actors perform, not the audience members.
- Do not encroach on anybody's personal space, including placing your feet on the seats in front of you, taking up arm-rests, excessive fidgeting or hanging a coat on the back of your seat.
- Avoid obstructing the view of others.

MUSEUMS AND GALLERIES

Being able to properly value and appreciate artistic and creative expression requires a certain amount of consideration from others so it is essential that certain rules and procedures are followed to create the best conditions possible for all concerned.

- Be observant and read the signs. If a sign says 'photography is prohibited', do not take photographs.
- Do not eat or drink in galleries or museums unless you are in a designated area.
- Be quiet. Limit the noise you make by whispering if you have to speak. Avoid shouting, laughing loudly and any making any other form of outburst at all times.
- Make an effort to understand the pieces you view, this will enhance your appreciation. If available, use an audio guide to gain a deeper understanding of the works and to help you navigate through the maze of art.
- Do not congregate in front of paintings in groups and discuss anything other than the art. This will be seen as selfish by other patrons waiting to view a particular piece.

GYM ETIQUETTE

Being a member of a gym has many benefits, some physical, some practical. As with every club, for any benefit to be gained, it is up to the individual to take responsibility for their contribution to the satisfaction of its members.

- Observe time limits on exercise machines during peak periods.

- Limit excessive noise including the kinds of grunts and outbursts that are synonymous with strenuous heavy lifting. This can be seen as boasting and may be off putting to others.
- Always apply antiperspirant deodorant before working out. Offensive body odor can completely ruin someone else's experience so be vigilant about personal hygiene and cleanliness.
- Use a towel to dry yourself between activities.
- Wipe down every surface on which you perspire with the appropriate cleaning agent if there is one provided. If not, simply wipe the surface with your towel.
- Arrive early to any exercise class for which the set-up of equipment is required.
- When partaking in a group activity such as a class, be mindful of others' personal space. Never sit so close to someone else that you make them feel uncomfortable. Use the distance between other people as a guide.
- Use a locker for your personal belongings. Carrying around a bag and placing it on the ground beside you can create a safety hazard for other members of the gym.
- Never drop weights or dumbbells.
- While waiting to use a machine, be subtle. Do not stand close enough to the person that you make them feel uneasy.
- When using communal changing rooms, be considerate of other people's tolerance to nudity. Be discreet after showering, always use a towel or a robe.
- Be aware that it is your responsibility to replace any equipment you use and return it to its rightful place when you have finished with it.

MEDICAL CENTER ETIQUETTE

It is highly likely that a trip to the Doctor is going to be unpleasant; lots of ill people being ill together in a waiting room—it's a grim scene. From the moment you arrive, be mindful not to consciously spread your germs around by sneezing, coughing, spluttering or belching without using a handkerchief or tissue to cover your mouth. If there is one thing that people should be selfish about, it's germs. Everyone is dealing with their own, nobody wants you to share yours. Be aware of your personal space and remain within it. Do not look over someone's shoulder at their reading material and do not point out or react to anybody's ailment or injury, no matter how shocking. Also, remember that people may be nervous in anticipation of receiving test results, they may even have had some bad news. For this reason it is important to maintain a quiet sense of calm, purely out of consideration for others. Avoid staring, striking up conversations with people, asking personal questions, eating and speaking loudly on your mobile phone. All of these things cause unnecessary tension and discomfort.

PLACES OF WORSHIP

From temples to churches and everything in between, when entering a place of worship, one should act in a manner that is respectful to the beliefs of that faith. Dress should be conservative and your manner should be one of quiet reverence. Upon entering a place of worship, regardless of whether or not you are religious, it is never appropriate to bring in refreshments such as take-away coffee. No food should be consumed at any time throughout the service. If you have to attend a religious ceremony where you are unfamiliar with the protocol, do your research ahead of time. Enquire about the appropriate dress and etiquette in order that you prevent causing accidental offence and make a good impression.

PUBLIC TRANSPORT ETIQUETTE

When using public transport it is vital that you demonstrate an understanding of the social conventions that are considered acceptable by the vast majority of people. Namely, keeping to one's self. This is considered polite as it ensures that everybody remains as comfortable as possible in an otherwise confined place crammed with strangers. Be aware of personal space, your own and that of others. Avoid staring at people and having loud conversations. Be mindful of the noise you are omitting and demonstrate an awareness of the fact that people may not wish to have their own headspace filled with whatever sounds may be belting out from within your headphones.

As a sign of respect, never hesitate to offer your seat if there is a person who may need it more that you. For example, if an elderly, frail, disabled or pregnant person is standing, regardless of your age or sex, you should offer your seat. Generally speaking, children and students should always give up their seats for adult passengers.

> *"For to be free is not merely to cast off one's chains, but to live in a*
> *way that respects and enhances the freedom of others."*
> —*Nelson Mandela*

AIR TRAVEL ETIQUETTE

Acting in a manner that demonstrates an awareness of others' personal space is essential when traveling by air, however, it is highly likely that your own personal space will be invaded at some point. Whether by a random elbow or a wandering eye, there are certain ways to deal with unwelcome space invasions.

All Aboard! Upon embarking, have your boarding pass ready so that the flight attendant may direct you to your seat. Once there, store your carry-on luggage in the overhead locker and take your seat as soon as possible. This shows that you are being considerate of others. If someone is in your allocated seat, double check that you have not made an error and politely inform them that they are sitting in the seat that has been allocated to you.

Chatterbox. If the person beside you is asking probing questions in an effort to engage you in discussion, by all means, go ahead. If you would prefer not to, begin to leaf through the pages of a book or magazine. As you become more absorbed, they should pick up on the subtle hint. Alternatively you could comment on how impressed you are by the quality of the inflight entertainment, casually put on your headset and snuggle in for some solitary serenity. Even if you aren't watching the screen, headphones are an excellent tool to use in any such situation.

Tight Squeeze. Never attempt to maneuver Cirque du Soleil style over a sleeping passenger as sudden turbulence could result in a not-so-subtle knee in the face. If the person sitting beside you falls asleep and you need to use the bathroom, lightly tap them on the shoulder and let them know. Violent invasions of personal space are never acceptable.

Things That Go 'Bump' in the Night. If you can feel the person behind you through the back of your seat, a child 'playing drums' on your head rest for instance, feel free to turn around and politely ask them to stop. If they do not, it is perfectly acceptable to ask the parent or guardian of that child to take control of the situation.

Germs. Always sneeze, cough or splutter into a handkerchief or tissue so as not to spread your germs around the cabin and if feeling nauseous, identify the whereabouts of the paper bag and ensure it is close at hand.

Following Instructions. Always follow the instructions given to you by the captain or members of the cabin crew without hesitation. This includes raising your seat to the upright position, putting on your seatbelt and switching off any electronic devices. This is important to ensure the comfort of the people around you.

Arrival. When it is time to disembark, as tempting as it is, try not to race to the door to be the first passenger off the plane. This can cause unnecessary chaos. Instead, calmly wait your turn and collect your belongings from the overhead compartment. Passing someone their bag if it is within arm's reach is a lovely gesture that demonstrates your willingness to assist others. You never know when you may need assistance, so try to go out of your way for people often. It builds character.

PASSENGER DO'S AND DON'TS

- Never encroach on another passenger's personal space.
- Avoid engaging in loud conversations.
- Ensure others cannot hear your music.
- Avoid the use of offensive language.
- Do not assume that people sitting beside you wish to have a discussion with you.
- Always cover your mouth when you sneeze, cough or splutter.
- Do not eat or drink on public transport other than for medical reasons.
- Never take up multiple seats on your own.
- Always give up your seat for someone less able bodied than yourself.
- Never place anybody on speakerphone within earshot of others.

SHOPPING ETIQUETTE

When shopping, it is important to recognize that while you may be indulging in a little retail therapy, you are doing so in somebody else's workplace. Always treat the sales clerk with respect. They are not your slave, nor are they being employed to deal with the rudeness of incessant shoppers who don't know any better. While browsing through the racks don't be rude by chatting loudly on your mobile phone, other people may not wish to listen to your private conversations. Sales staff are required to make sure you leave a satisfied customer so do think about the way you like to be treated at work and act accordingly.

Scoffing at the Price. Scoffing at the price of something because you don't recognize the name of the designer is rude. In the same way that you wouldn't walk into a boutique and exclaim 'That's not worth that much money!' you shouldn't make snide remarks about the prices of things under your breath. Quite simply, if you find yourself perplexed at a price tag, replace the item and move on until you find something more suitable.

Children. While some stores are more tolerant of children than others, it remains the responsibility of the parents to control them. Allowing children to try clothes on for fun may seem harmless enough but in reality, they are simply making more work for the sales assistant. Moreover, it is not really appropriate for children to be handling expensive items that may be easily damaged or broken.

Fitting Rooms. Queuing for a fitting room can be time consuming in a busy store. For this reason, never try on clothes you have no intension of buying as it is a waste of everyone's time. Once inside, be mindful of the time you take out of consideration for the people still waiting in the queue. Never leave the clothes you try on in crumpled piles on the floor. If you wouldn't do that with your own clothes, don't do it to somebody else's. When you have finished, hang each of the items neatly back on their hangers and hand them to the sales assistant.

Over the Top. Contrary to popular belief, being opposed to waiting in queues does not give anyone exclusive rights to try on items of clothing over the top of their own on the shop floor. Attempting to squeeze into items in this way not only causes damage, but diminishes the image of the store. If you are time poor, come back to the store another day rather than trying to cut corners.

Workload. As you look through racks of clothes ensure you replace items neatly back where you found them. Be aware that every item you pick up and replace will have to be adjusted by the sales assistant as soon as you leave, so don't go out of your way to make their work more difficult than is has to be.

Food. Never take food or drink into a clothing store or boutique. If there isn't a sign, assume that it's an unspoken rule. Spills, crumbs and dirty fingers make food and shopping a risky combination for both the proprietor and the customer. If you stain or damage an item of clothing in a store, signage or not, it will be your responsibility to pay for that item.

Pets. A day out with your pooch or parrot can be wonderful providing you aren't going shopping. Taking an animal into a store is uncouth and should be avoided at all times. Aside from the potential damage that could be caused to the stock (which you would be required to replace), you aren't in a position to gauge the impact your animal may have on other people. Remember, animals aren't for everybody so stick to the park.

Toilet Stop. Some stores have bathrooms for the comfort of their staff and clientele. For this reason, one should always treat bathrooms in stores as private, never assuming that they are for public use. This means that if you need to use a bathroom and find yourself running into the nearest boutique to do so, it would be appropriate to make a post-pee purchase. If not, there are plenty of public bathrooms to choose from.

SHOPPING DO'S AND DON'TS

- Never disrespect, talk down to, patronize or belittle sales staff. This sort of behavior would be an immediate reflection of the poor quality of your character.
- Be polite at all times and respond to friendly greetings appropriately. If you walk into a store and are greeted with a friendly 'Hello', a response is absolutely required.
- If you wish to be left to browse, do not be gruff with staff when they ask if you need assistance, simply say 'thank you' and tell them that you are 'happy to browse'.

- Bathe and apply deodorant before heading off to buy clothing. If you have been to the gym for instance, refrain from shopping for clothes so that you don't rub your perspiration all over clothes that you may not purchase.
- Treat every item you touch with care and be mindful of the fact that you are liable for any damaged items.
- Do not use the furniture in a store to take a rest unless you are waiting for somebody in the fitting room who intends to make a purchase.

DINING ETIQUETTE

"The world was my oyster but I used the wrong fork."
—*Oscar Wilde*

Sharing a meal with others is a universal practice that can mark the most casual of get-togethers as well as the most ceremonious of events. Understanding the various intricacies of meal-time behavior is not only culturally significant, but important for all members of a community to feel as though they belong. Meals facilitate sharing, bonding and learning through discussion. A lot can be revealed about a person by the way that they conduct themselves during a meal, which makes it a good opportunity to make an excellent first impression. Familiarizing yourself with the following elements of dining etiquette, will help you to feel confident and comfortable in any social situation.

CONTEMPORARY TABLE MANNERS

Whether eating and drinking in a formal or casual setting, demonstrating good manners is the first step to ensuring people are at ease in your company. Showing that you care about others' needs sends a clear message about who you are and reflects high personal standards.

- Put your phone away. Never use your phone at the table, regardless of whether you are using it as a phone, a camera or a computer. Never send a text message, show someone something on your screen, tweet, send an email or look up information. Attempting to do these things, however discreetly, will be considered the height of rudeness by others in your company.
- Avoid taking photographs of yours or anybody else's meal.
- Keep your elbows off the table.
- Never pick your teeth. If the need arises, excuse yourself and do so in the bathroom.
- Chew with your mouth closed and never speak if you have food in your mouth.
- Err on the side of caution when it comes to topics of conversation and keep controversial opinions to yourself.
- Use cutlery and glassware appropriately.
- In larger groups, make an effort to speak to the people on either side of you rather than shouting across the table.
- Do not begin eating until everybody has taken their seat. If a host is present, wait until they begin unless otherwise instructed.
- Do not help yourself to anybody else's food.
- Always ask for something to be passed to you if it is out of your immediate reach. Salt and pepper should always be passed together regardless of which one has been requested.
- Butter knives are for butter only. Bread should always be broken so use your hands to break bread into bite-sized pieces before buttering.

- While pausing between bites, rest your knife and fork on the plate as indicated in the diagram. Once used, cutlery should not be rested on the table top for any reason.
- Unless you are a child under ten, do not cut up your meal first and proceed to use your fork as a shovel. Always use your knife and fork together to cut small pieces of food before bringing the fork to your mouth and always eat from the top of the fork—yes, even where peas are concerned! Alternatively, if mashed potato is served with peas, it is acceptable to use it as a glue with which to fasten the peas to the fork.
- If eating soup, always push the spoon away from yourself and bring the spoon to your mouth rather than leaning down over the bowl. Sip rather than slurp the soup from the spoon. Between mouthfuls, rest the spoon on the plate beneath the bowl.
- Avoid waving your cutlery around. You will be perceived as being a utensil-wielding maniac.
- Never lick your fingers. Ever.
- Make an effort not to make loud crunching, slurping, smacking or gnawing noises while you eat.
- Always pass food to the right.
- Never use your napkin as a handkerchief or a bib by tucking it into your clothes.
- Always pass items to others with the handle facing outwards.

THE USE OF CUTLERY

Continental Style. Widely accepted as the style of choice outside of America, the Continental Style of dining involves the knife being held in the right hand and the fork in the left throughout the duration of the meal. The tines of the fork should face downwards while bite-sized pieces of food are cut and placed into one's mouth accordingly. To drink, place both the knife and fork in the resting position. To do this, cross your fork over the top of the knife with the tines facing downward as indicated in the diagram below. Conversely, upon completion of your meal, place your cutlery side by side at twelve o'clock in the center of the plate with the tines of the fork facing downward.

American Style. This style of eating differs slightly from the Continental Style in that once a bite sized piece of food has been cut, it is acceptable to put the knife down and take the fork into the right hand before using it to bring food to your mouth. Depending on the food, when holding the fork in the right hand, it may not be necessary to keep the tines facing downward.

Resting

Finished

INFORMAL DINING ETIQUETTE

In a situation where a less formal style of dining is required, such as a casual dinner with close friends, a barbeque or buffet style arrangement, the above rules would still apply. However there are some other things you need to be aware of. Firstly, never push in front of anybody waiting in a queue. When serving yourself, the amount of food you put on your plate should be directly proportionate to the amount of food you intend to eat. Never pile your plate sky-high at a buffet and risk being labeled rude and greedy. Also, once you have put food on your plate, you cannot change your mind and put it back.

Use the serving utensils provided and do not touch any of the food with your hands. Whenever finger food is served, avoid double dipping at all costs. This may be off-putting to other dip enthusiasts who do not necessarily wish the dip to be tainted by your half-gnawed carrot nub. Dipping enhances the flavor of the item being dipped, not the other way around. Do not use food such as carrot sticks or crackers as a vehicle for which to shovel vast amounts of dip into your mouth.

FORMAL DINING ETIQUETTE

Although the very thought of formal dining makes some people anxious, but do not be afraid, the rules exist for the purpose of making everybody feel comfortable. To begin, sit up straight with your legs evenly placed on the ground in front of you and place your hands in your lap. Place your napkin on your lap and if you need to leave the table mid-meal for any reason, excuse yourself and place the napkin on the left side of your place setting.

When dining out, do not begin until everybody at the table has a meal in front of them. If the meal is being served by the host, wait until they are seated before you begin, unless otherwise instructed to do so. If the dishes are presented in the center of the table, never serve yourself first, be attentive to the requests of others around you. Ask for anything that you need rather than reaching for it and use 'please' and 'thank you' often. Eat your food at a moderate pace so as not to appear famished or to cause the host any inconvenience by lagging between courses. Place your cutlery in the resting position when drinking and always sip, rather than slurp from the glass. If wine or champagne is served, hold glasses by the stem.

RESTAURANT ETIQUETTE

When it comes to eating out, it is customary for the person that invited the guests to be responsible for the bill, however, in cases where large groups of friends are getting together, splitting the bill in a restaurant would be far more appropriate. If you have been invited to dinner, it does not necessarily mean you should order the most expensive item on the menu. This would be an example of bad manners. If the person with whom you are dining simply orders soup, avoid selecting the most expensive cut of steak available. Regardless of your financial situation, it is courteous to consider others when making your food and beverage selections.

Never whistle, call out, clink cutlery against glassware or wave your hands to get the attention of a waiter. It would be the height of rudeness to do so. Instead, make eye contact and slightly raise your index finger. As they approach, start by saying 'excuse me' before asking any questions. If they greet you first, politely respond. Usually, an open menu suggests that you have not yet made a selection. If you have and are waiting to be served, close the menu as a signal that you are ready to order. If your waiter is particularly attentive and has approached you before you have made a decision, avoid having them wait while you do so. Instead, politely ask them to give you a few extra minutes to decide.

NAVIGATING A TABLE SETTING

Now that you're a dining etiquette aficionado, how do you navigate the complex maze of the table setting? This process need not be difficult. Once mastered, the following guide will make smooth sailing out of dining and have you well on your way to becoming the perfect host.

A simple trick is to remember the letters BMW. From left to right, the most humble of table settings requires Bread, a Meal and some Water. Using this as a starting point, you can expand your horizons to more complex arrangements. Forks are placed on the left of the plate, while knives and spoons are placed on the right. When trying to ascertain which utensil to use when, remember to work from the outside in. The smaller fork on the outside is for the entrée or salad, while the middle set of cutlery is for the main meal. The only other utensils that should be to the right of the knife are a teaspoon, a soupspoon and/or a cocktail fork. A dessert fork should be placed above your plate underneath a dessert spoon. When the dessert is served these utensils should be slid down to the side of the plate, the spoon to the right and the fork to the left. Use the fork to push bite sized pieces of the dessert onto the spoon before bringing the spoon to your mouth to eat. If you are in a restaurant, any utensils that are not required should be removed by the waiter. When dining in someone's home, use the utensils as a guide to establish how many courses will be served.

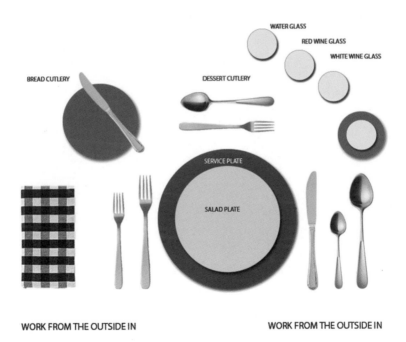

Formal table setting

AFTERNOON TEA ETIQUETTE

Afternoon Tea is a British tradition, stemming from the Duchess of Bedford's desire to quash her hunger pangs between lunch and dinner. Since then, taking afternoon tea has become popular in many cultures. Generally served at four o'clock, afternoon tea consists of sandwiches, scones and preserves and a selection of cakes. However, there are a few variations on the traditional afternoon tea such as the Cream Tea and the Royal Tea. During a Cream Tea, only scones and preserves are served with the tea, and a Royal Tea consists of a glass of champagne in addition to the usual assortment of scones, sandwiches and cakes. When taking tea, it is essential that one demonstrates impeccable manners and conveys an understanding of correct afternoon tea etiquette. It is a tradition after all!

1. Take the napkin and place it on your lap with the crease facing inward. If wearing lipstick, it is also acceptable for a lady to have the crease facing away from her in order that she may hide any stains that may have appeared on the napkin after wiping her mouth.
2. Tea should be poured into the teacup before the milk and stirred once, clockwise from the bottom to the top of the cup. The spoon should then be placed delicately into the saucer.
3. When eating scones, begin by initiating the passing around of the jam and cream.
4. Next, place a small amount of jam and cream onto your own plate rather than poking your knife repeatedly into the smaller dishes.

5. As with bread, break off small pieces of the scone with your hands, atop which you would spread jam and cream. In the UK, the Cornish tradition is to spread the jam first, followed by a dollop of cream, but in Devon the tradition is to dollop the jam over the cream. If enjoying afternoon tea outside of those places, the order of jam and cream simply comes down to personal preference! Never dunk anything into your tea or lick your fingers. Ever.

6. A smart casual dress code should apply to any afternoon tea taken in the company of guests or in public.

PARTIES, FUNCTIONS
AND FORMAL OCCASIONS

"Don't reserve your best behavior for special occasions.
You can't have two sets of manners, two social codes— one for
those you admire and want to impress, another for those whom you
consider unimportant. You must be the same to all people."
—Lillian Eichler Watson

HOST ETIQUETTE

There are many factors to consider when hosting a successful party. Whether a cocktail party, a casual get together or a dinner party, it is important that your guests feel comfortable and entertained throughout. This can be quite a challenge if you aren't familiar with all that is required of you. The following guidelines will help you master the art of becoming the perfect host and ensure your guests have a wonderful time.

- First of all, you need to think about a guest list. Once it is complete, formally invite your guests at least three weeks in advance and be sure to include an RSVP date.
- The host is responsible for providing the food and drinks so ensure you are aware of any special dietary requirements your

guests may have. Keep in mind that it is appropriate when serving alcohol to also provide a selection of non-alcoholic beverages.

- Greeting your guests as they arrive is another duty of the host. Take their bags and coats and place them in a designated area.
- Be sure to thank them warmly for any gifts they may bring you and introduce them to anybody already present.
- Next, point them in the direction of the refreshments.
- Ensure there is an adequate number of glasses and napkins etc. For the duration of the party, make sure the food and drinks are replenished accordingly.
- If serving foods that cannot be fully consumed, such as olives or snacks on cocktail sticks, having little bowls to place such waste into is a good idea. You don't want your guests to have to carry olive pits around with them.
- If you are hosting a sit down meal, have a seating plan with males and females seated beside one another. This makes for interesting discussion and prevents the table being divided into gender groups.

THE INVITATION CHECK LIST

- Send invitations no less than three weeks in advance.
- State the occasion.
- Include an RSVP date.
- State the dress code required and give any extra detail you feel is appropriate or necessary.
- Include an option to specify whether guests have any special

dietary requirements.
- Include a start and end time for the event.
- Include a map or written directions to the address.
- Include your contact details in order that people may respond appropriately.

GUEST ETIQUETTE

Parties are a great way to meet people, make new friends and strengthen bonds with existing ones. Most people like to socialize and being the perfect guest at a party is the best way of making sure you are invited to many more.
- Make an effort to RSVP as soon as you can. This gives the host adequate time to cater for the number of guests attending. If you can't attend for some reason, it is always better to personally inform the host rather than to simply not make an appearance.
- Never arrive early. This shows complete disregard for the host who will surely be busy with preparations.
- Always bring a gift to acknowledge the efforts of the host but avoid anything that may give them extra work such as flowers. Although lovely, they need to be put into water immediately and trying to locate a vase may inconvenience the host. A book or some chocolates would be appropriate gifts, as would a bottle of wine (age permitting).
- Do not attempt to consume any wine or chocolate that you may have brought along. A gift is a gift.
- Upon arrival, if you haven't been greeted by the host, your first

task should be to find and greet them. Once you have made your presence known, try to mingle with the other guests.

– If a person approaches you, proceed with introductions accordingly and never leave anybody standing on their own. Even if they have the conversational prowess of an hors d'oeuvre, wait until you have introduced them to somebody else before excusing yourself.

– If you are of age and alcohol is provided, avoid becoming intoxicated. It will make you appear foolish and greedy. By eating and drinking only your fair share, you are demonstrating consideration for the other guests.

– If you spill anything, inform the host immediately and help clean up. Similarly, if you break anything, assure the host you will replace it and be true to your word.

– Be sure to thank the host before leaving rather than executing the perfect disappearing act. It is polite to acknowledge the effort they have gone to in providing you a good time.

– Never overstay your welcome by being the last guest at a party. This places the host in an awkward position as it would be rude to ask you to leave.

THE DANGERS

Everyone loves a party right? Right. Getting ready with the girls, looking amazing, walking in to find potential suitors everywhere— it's a dream come true. So how does a girl get noticed for the right reasons? The answer is simple and the very first thing to work on is maintaining control. Getting noticed takes a lot of work when you think about it. First of all, you need to be confident and mingle with everyone. No one finds the nervously giggling jelly pot in the corner attractive. You need to pass up offers of alcohol because this will sabotage all the effort you have put into looking fabulous. Also, you must never drink wine from a box—no matter how cool you think you are, drinking wine from a box is not chic, it is cheap.

Whether it's your own party or someone else's, you need to know that becoming intoxicated creeps up on you and can knock you down without any warning whatsoever. If this happens, you will lose all control of your body and even worse, all control of the impression you are making on others. If you collapse in a vomiting heap on the bathroom floor at a party, it is highly likely that everyone will see you being escorted from the premises and you will be haunted (for the rest of your days) by some kind of nickname that when said, reminds everyone of how terrible you looked being dragged away.

I know this all sounds dramatic. In fact, you're probably even having an 'as if that would ever happen to me' moment, right? Well it does happen. It happens all the time and it could easily be you that it happens to if you let it. Have you ever seen what vomiting can do to perfectly applied makeup? It can make the prettiest girl look like a circus attraction, the most chic of hairstyles look like a compost heap and even the most waterproof mascara will creep over every inch of your face. There are only two words to describe this situation—NOT ATTRACTIVE.

So you're in center of a significant dilemma; all of a sudden your brain is telling you to do rebellious things because it's fun and it will increase your cool 'it-girl' vibe by infinity. You like to think of yourself as having it all together but really, inside you're stressing about what everyone thinks of you. The problem is that often, girls try so hard to be accepted that they'll do just about anything to attain acceptance. Feeling the need to belong is a craving that will dwarf any bag or shoe fantasy that anyone has ever had. As you may already know, this need can manifest in various forms including doing the inconceivable, saying the unbelievable, letting a someone treat you like a piece of meat or worse, a piece of trash, being horrible to someone less cool than you and various other things that you will regret later on.

Whatever it is that you do to get acceptance, make sure it doesn't diminish your self-respect. Losing this will significantly reduce your chances of being respected. If you're out and everybody is drinking it's more than likely you will want to join in:

A) because you don't want people to think you are a loser

B) because you want to up your general cool factor.

Unfortunately, the second you have a little too much, you risk being 'that girl' who spewed all over so-and-so's parents' new lounge—or worse! Scarily, there's a very fine line between being cool and being an outcast. Think about it; you're trying your best to be cool, gorgeous, confident and popular, but choosing to do things that could end all your hard work quicker than a rumor spreading around school. Why? If being drunk and having your best friend hold your hair back while you vomit in front of everyone makes even the prettiest girl look ugly!

EMERGENCY ETIQUETTE

Sometimes things just don't go to plan. In these tricky situations, a thorough understanding of the best way to go about dealing with things is invaluable. It is important to note here that in most situations, using sensible judgment and maturity is the best way forward. Take a New Year's Eve party for example, if someone has opened their home to a large number of guests, various other factors may combine to heighten the risk of trouble occurring. Always make every possible attempt to remove yourself from any situation that makes you feel uncomfortable or uneasy. Trust your instincts, phone someone and make arrangements to get yourself home.

UNDER THE INFLUENCE

Being under the influence of anything means you have had too much of it. It is at this point where normal judgment becomes impaired, along with the ability to make quick or sensible decisions. This is why so many people risk their lives by attempting to drive after having consumed alcohol. Whatever the reason may be, it is vital that you remain alert at all times in any social situation in order to reduce the risk of making poor decisions that could impact the rest of your life.

If you see someone collapse or become unconscious and you know that they have been involved in excessive drinking, always call or phone for help. If in doubt, call an ambulance without delay. Usually, the trained professional on the other end of the line will be able to gauge the level of response required, so it is always better to phone and establish if an ambulance is not needed than having to spend your entire life wondering.

SAFE PARTYING DO'S AND DON'TS

- Never take recreational drugs. You don't know what they are made of or how they will affect you physically or psychologically.
- Do not binge drink. It will significantly diminish the control you have over what you do and what you say.
- Do not let your friends drive if they have been drinking. If you have to take or hide their keys, do so.
- Never get into a car with an intoxicated person if that person is intending to drive the vehicle. If you can't stop them from doing so, stop yourself.
- Never hesitate to call the police if you or others are in danger.
- Never hesitate to call for an ambulance in an emergency or suspected emergency.
- Avoid walking alone at night through unsafe, unfamiliar or poorly lit places.
- Always ensure somebody you trust knows exactly where you are at all times.

THE BELLE OF THE BALL

Being asked to a formal or ball by a boy can be amazing, especially if he's prospective boyfriend material. Even if you're just great friends, it's sure to be a great night out and can be a fabulous boost to your self-esteem. Just the thought of shopping for the perfect dress, getting your hair and makeup done and pin-pointing that amazing pair of shoes is enough to up the excitement level of even the most drab of weeks.

There is one thing, though, that could turn your dream formal into a nightmare—getting drunk. Whether this happens at the lucky fellow's pre-drinks (that your parents finally agreed to let you go to), or at the formal itself, this is the worst thing you could ever do! Getting drunk can creep up on you without any warning. When you're drunk you can lose control of your actions and choices which will effect the impression that people have of you. If you collapse in a vomiting heap on the bathroom floor at a formal, it's more than likely that a female teacher, or someone's mother will hear or see you and have you sent home. How embarrassing!

WEDDING GUEST ETIQUETTE

Weddings are a call for celebration and as such, being a guest at a wedding can be a lot of fun. In order that a wedding is enjoyable for all who attend, demonstrating a thorough understanding of the correct etiquette is essential for the overall success of the event.

RSVP. Be sure to respond to a wedding invitation as soon as you can so as to avoid forgetting or misplacing the invitation. This is crucial in terms of showing respect for the preparation that the bride and groom will have put into planning the event. Be sure to complete the entire form which should ask you to indicate whether or not you have any food allergies etc.

Plus One. If the invitation has only your name written on it, then it is safe to presume that you, and only you, have been invited. Never phone the bride or groom and ask to bring a partner as this would put them in a very awkward situation. The only exception to this rule is if a person's fiancée, husband or wife has been omitted from the invitation. In cases such as this, it is likely to be an oversight on the bride or groom's behalf as married or engaged couples should always be considered as one. If this occurs, it is perfectly acceptable to politely remind the bride or groom of your significant other.

The Ceremony. Opting out of the ceremony in favor of the reception is unacceptable. If you accept a wedding invitation it is polite to commit to all components of the celebration.

Timing is Everything. Though wedding ceremonies tend to run a few minutes later than scheduled, it is important for guests to arrive at least 20 minutes early. Regardless of the venue, plan ahead of time to ensure you are organized regarding modes of transport, parking and seating. Often, parking can be difficult due to the number of guests who may be trying to park as close as possible to the venue.

Seating. If there appear to be less seats than there are guests, it should be assumed that the seating is reserved for the immediate family of the bride and groom only. During the ceremony itself, ensure your phone is switched off and that you do not talk, laugh or make outbursts of any kind. Behaving in a manner that detracts from the bride and groom is considered rude and will be remembered by other guests well into the future. Do not eat or drink or chew gum during any part of the ceremony.

Confetti. As the bride and groom walk down the aisle together for the first time as husband and wife, it may be appropriate to throw flower petals or confetti. If the marriage has taken place indoors, wait until the bride and groom are outside before throwing anything into the air. In some cultures, it is customary to throw grains of rice at a newly married couple. This practice stems from ancient times and served as a symbol of fertility and prosperity for the newlyweds. If you are given grains of rice to throw, remember that it is intended as a symbolic gesture rather than an all-out attack! A grain of rice in the eye of the bride could potentially ruin one of the most important days of her life so err on the side of caution.

The Reception: Mind the Gap. Usually there is a gap between a wedding ceremony and the reception in which the bridal party have a series of professional photographs taken. Whether there has been something planned for guests in the interim or not, it important to arrive at the reception venue on time to witness the formal entrance and introduction of the bridal party and the newly betrothed couple. It is polite to listen attentively to the Master of Ceremonies as they address the formalities of the occasion.

Dress Code. As a guest, you must never dress in a manner that upstages the bride on her wedding day. This includes but is not limited to outfits that are overly revealing or inappropriately provocative in any way and wearing white or cream. Guests should strictly adhere to the dress code stipulated on the invitation. If you are unsure, it is perfectly acceptable to phone the bride in advance to enquire about the suitability of certain attire. In any case, aim to look elegant.

Gifts. A wedding gift is symbolic of well wishes, appreciation and abundance for the new couple as they begin a life together. It is important to note that while purchasing a gift from the bridal registry is not compulsory, it is tasteful to put some thought into your selection. Do some research and purchase a gift that you think the couple will like. The time and care you put into your selection will not only be appreciated by the couple, it will represent the importance you place on your relationship with them. If in doubt, remember that it is always more tasteful to give a thoughtful gift within your means than a small amount of money in a card.

Photography and Social Media. The bride and groom will have spent a lot of time and effort selecting a professional photographer to capture their special day. For this reason alone, it is inconsiderate to use your phone to take photographs for the purpose of publishing them on social media. In addition, memorable events are always better experienced in person rather than from behind the lens of a camera, so make an effort to be fully present. There is however, an exception to the rule: If the bride and groom have requested that photos be taken and published to a social media platform such as Instagram under a particular hashtag, then by all means do so. The fundamental principles of etiquette are essentially about demonstrating respect for others, so if the bride and groom have a special request, the appropriate action would be to gracefully oblige.

Phones. Mobile phones should be switched off or be set to silent mode for the duration of the event. If you need to check for messages, from a babysitter for instance, it would be appropriate to do so in the bathroom.

Children. Some couples may elect to label their wedding day a 'child free' zone in which case, all guests should gracefully oblige. If alternative childcare arrangements cannot be made, it is perfectly acceptable to decline the invitation. It is never acceptable to ask the bride or groom if they will make an exception for your children. This places them under an unnecessary amount of stress and may cause awkwardness or conflict. If children have been invited, they should be supervised at all times.

Alcohol. Over consumption of alcohol is never acceptable. If alcohol has been provided at a wedding celebration, age permitting, by all means enjoy a drink. However, over consumption of anything simply because it is free is distasteful and uncouth, so avoid binge drinking and becoming intoxicated at all costs. Not only will it diminish your experience of the event, it may cause you to lose control of yourself and behave in a manner that you may regret in the future. Having to two or more drinks at a time in order that you need not go back and forth from the bar is obnoxious and disrespectful to the married couple and their respective parents. If you find that your champagne flute has been filled, assume it is for an upcoming toast and refrain from drinking it until that time.

Mingling. It is polite to speak with the people either side of you at your table and appropriate to mingle with other guests throughout the duration of the wedding. Before leaving, ensure you introduce yourself to the parents of the bride and groom and thank them for having you at such a special event. At some stage, the newlyweds will make their way around the venue to mingle with their guests. When they pass by, congratulate them, comment on how beautiful the bride looks and make a statement that indicates the wonderful time you are having. Do not ask them any questions or spend time chatting as this may significantly prolong the process.

Dining. Weddings are formal events so the demonstration of impeccable table manners and an understanding of formal dining etiquette is essential (see: Chapter 8—Dining Etiquette).

Speeches and Toasting. During the speeches, it is appropriate to be silent and listen attentively to each of the speakers. Try not to leave the table during the speeches as this is considered to be extremely rude behavior. Most people become anxious at the mere thought of speaking before a group, let alone having to deliver a formal speech in front of hundreds of people at a wedding! For this reason alone, show respect to the speakers and respond appropriately to the toasts. (See: Chapter 6—Social Graces)

Catching the Bouquet. At some point in the evening, all the single ladies will be asked to assemble in front of the bride who will throw her bouquet into the air. Traditionally, it was thought that the lucky lady who caught the bouquet would be the next in line to be wed.

Wedding Favors/Bonbonniere. The wedding favor or bonbonniere is a small gift from the bride and groom to keep as a memento of their special day. It is considered polite to remember to take it with you upon leaving the venue as a lot of time and effort will have gone into its selection. It is also important to note that it would be in extremely poor taste to take anything else with you from the room. Looting is never chic! Contrary to popular belief, the flower arrangements and centerpieces are not yours for the taking.

FUNERAL ETIQUETTE

Attending a funeral demands the demonstration of utmost respect for others. Your presence acknowledges the life of someone that has passed away and is symbolic of your support for the grieving.

Dress Code. Unless otherwise instructed by the family of the deceased, the dress code for funerals is conservative. Traditionally, wearing black is a symbol of sympathy and mourning and is appropriate in most cases. However, wearing subdued, dark tones is also acceptable, provided the attire is neat, tidy and uncomplicated. Avoid clothing that is revealing or provocative in any way; you should never aim to draw attention to yourself at a funeral.

Punctuality. It is important that you arrive early so as not to interrupt the service. Plan ahead of time and ensure you have organized transport and parking etc.

Be Seated. When you arrive, be seated immediately rather than attempting to seek out the immediate family to whom you wish to pay your respects. This can cause a queue as others will try to follow your lead. If you wish to personally give your condolences, do wait for the appropriate time in order to prevent unnecessary delays.

Mobile Phones. If you haven't done so already, once you have taken your seat, turn your mobile phone off to prevent any interruptions to the service.

Food. Do not consume any food or drink during a funeral service.

Conduct. Your demeanor should reflect the somber nature of the occasion. It is therefore highly inappropriate to laugh, chat, point or cause any disruption to the service.

Displays of Emotion. It is perfectly normal to feel emotional at a funeral so ensure you are prepared by taking a handkerchief or a small packet of tissues with you. If you begin to cry, do not be alarmed, this is a normal human reaction to sadness. However, if for some reason or other your crying becomes uncontrollable or loud, it would be appropriate to discreetly move outside or away from the congregation until such time as you have composed yourself.

Condolences. At some funerals, the immediate family gather together in order that the congregation may pay their respects personally. This usually occurs at the end of the service and prior to the burial or cremation. If the family form a line, you should take the opportunity to talk to them before proceeding to the burial. Do remember that it is not a party so any behavior that may be seen as irreverent is to be avoided.

The Burial. Many services consist of two parts, the ceremony and the burial or cremation. If the funeral procession moves on to the cemetery, it is correct etiquette to attend.

Priority Seating. Always be aware that the immediate relatives of the deceased take priority over everybody else. This includes any seating that may be available at the burial or cremation.

Respect. Do continue to demonstrate appropriate behavior by remaining composed, respectful quiet and reflective. Never behave in a manner that may detract from the purpose of the occasion. If in a cemetery, do not lean on any headstones or walk over any graves. Stay on the allocated paths and be aware of the people around you at all times.

Photography. Photography is inappropriate and unacceptable at a funeral service of any kind.

FORMAL OCCASION DO'S AND DON'TS

- Demonstrate impeccable manners at all times.
- Observe the dress code.
- Refrain from using foul or offensive language and avoid speaking about any subject matter that may be considered controversial or scandalous.
- Never become intoxicated.
- Respect the guests of honor by acting in a manner that shows respect for others.
- Do not be the last to leave.
- Do not leave before any of the formalities have taken place.
- Mingle with other guests.
- Do not draw unnecessary attention to yourself.
- Be present. Do not call, text, email, tweet, post, take photographs with or play games on your phone.
- Do not partake in any illegal activities whatsoever.
- Remain fully clothed at all times. At no stage should you ever need to remove your shoes, or anything else.
- Never openly seduce, inappropriately touch or harass another person.

CHAPTER 10

RELATIONSHIPS

"There are three possible parts to a date, of which at least two must be offered: entertainment, food and affection. It is customary to begin a series of dates with a great deal of entertainment, a moderate amount of food, and the merest suggestion of affection. As the amount of affection increases, the entertainment can be reduced proportionately. When the affection IS the entertainment, we no longer call it dating. Under no circumstances can the food be omitted."
—*Judith Martin*

THE DATING GAME

Dates are a great way of getting to know somebody more intimately and they allow you to assess whether or not you would be compatible in a relationship. When dating, there are a few important things to remember such as keeping an open mind and having enough confidence to be yourself. Appearing as though you are comfortable in your own skin is an attractive quality to have and, when coupled with the demonstration of good manners, creates a strong platform from which good impressions can be made.

The first thing to note when being asked on a date, is that it is polite to either gladly accept or politely decline the invitation. Never say 'maybe'or that you 'will think about it.'Agood general rule is to treat other people as you would like to be treated in the same situation. Consider how it would feel if you had mustered up the courage to ask someone on a date and they declined in a way that didn't take your feelings into account? Being well mannered is always important in situations where people's feelings are involved so make sure you tread lightly, keeping the other person's dignity intact is paramount. Never laugh or scoff at someone's advances, if they are genuinely interested in you, you should be flattered and remain polite at all times. However, being polite doesn't mean sacrificing your standards. Trust your instincts, you are not obliged to do anything you do not wish to do. If you feel uncomfortable for any reason, you should act accordingly by removing yourself from the situation.

Next, you need to consider what sort of people you are going to allow into your life by thinking about your expectations. If you aren't sure, think about the qualities you deem to be important in a person and apply the same set of standards to those with whom you're considering spending your time. Having similar standards, and values in common is an excellent start to any relationship. Write a list. You know very well what you like when it comes to clothes and accessories, so start working out what sort of qualities a person has to have for you to even consider looking at them—twice.

As you get better at this skill, you will be able to spot a fake from a mile away. Reading the signs is easy, if a person takes care of themselves, they have a sense of pride. If they have a good relationship with their parents and siblings, it says a lot about their character and personality. If they have a mixed group of close friends, they're probably kind and loyal. The list goes on and on. Another important factor to consider in terms of prospective relationship potential is what you don't want. Some qualities are enough to cancel out any good ones, for example:a bad reputation; drug taking; violent tendencies when drunk, or worse, when sober; known to be a sleaze or breaker of hearts; convicted criminal; ill-mannered and the list goes on and on. The important thing is that you learn to identify these things before you even consider any kind of relationship.

There is no such thing as being too selective when it comes to the qualities you find attractive in someone's personality, so never settle for somebody if you aren't certain about whether your values are aligned. When you are shopping for a new outfit for the weekend, you are very particular right? Even if you don't have much money, you still wouldn't stoop so low as to buy something your grandmother would wear simply because it was all you could afford. Well unfortunately, too many girls are settling for the 'grandmother clothes' of the dating pool because their self-esteem purse is empty. Don't settle for the last dress on the rack, EVER! It probably won't fit properly, a button, bow or zip will end up annoying you and you will end up feeling stupid because under normal circumstances, you 'wouldn't be seen dead in that dress'! The same principle applies to people; don't make do because their obvious interest makes you feel good about yourself. Even if all your friends have partners and you feel left out, never settle for anyone that doesn't fulfill your own requirements. You will end up feeling uncomfortable and lonely.

DATING DO'S AND DON'TS

- If you agree to meet somebody at a certain time and place, be there. Never leave somebody waiting.
- Always be on time, waiting alone could make a person feel awkward, uncertain and uncomfortable.
- If you are running late, call or text the person waiting for you. It shows that you have considered their feelings.
- If for some reason you can no longer make the date, phone the person as far in advance as possible and try to postpone rather than canceling all together.
- If the other person is obviously going to a lot of effort to make you feel special, acknowledge their gestures by saying thank you.
- If food is involved and you have the luxury of being able to choose it, choose wisely. Avoid anything that you may feel nervous or uncomfortable eating such as spaghetti or salad.
- Never divulge too much personal information on a first date, it may cause the other person to feel uncomfortable.
- Avoid talking obsessively about yourself, instead, politely ask questions that allow you to get a good idea about the sorts of things you may or may not have in common.
- When walking through a crowd, it is considered polite for the male to take the lead but in a restaurant or theater, the male should step aside for the lady to take her seat.
- Do not swear, become intoxicated or behave in a manner that may be considered offensive.
- Never abandon your date, always stay until the end.
- If payment is required, usually the male offers, especially if he

initiated the date. If this is the case, offer to contribute to some of the cost, for example, perhaps you may offer to pay for the popcorn if he paid for the tickets. If he insists, graciously accept by saying thank you.

– Maintain eye contact during conversations.
– Be sincere, honest and genuine. Avoid lying or conveying an image of yourself that is inaccurate. For instance, never say you enjoy sports if you don't. Being an individual is attractive and interesting.
– Be well mannered. The way you treat others is a fairly accurate indication of the type of person you are, so treating others with respect and dignity is important.
– Avoid physical intimacy on a first date. A hug or kiss on the cheek would be appropriate.

THE ONE

"However so much as you are capable of doing,
dare to do that much."
—*Thomas Aquinas*

Being in a romantic relationship usually means that you have made a commitment to be faithful to someone who has made the same commitment to you. After a period of dating, a relationship becomes exclusive or it doesn't. If the two people concerned have mutually strong feelings for one another, this will occur, if not, the frequency of dates will dwindle or cease all together. The following three principals are central to the success of any relationship.

Trust. Trust is a major factor, without it, a relationship cannot progress. When you are committed to someone, you are virtually downloading each other's personal details, thoughts, hopes and fears—you're effectively signing over your heart! Therefore you need to be certain the other person will do everything in their power not to break it and vice versa. If someone develops feelings for another outside of the relationship, it is their obligation to end the relationship immediately.

Honesty. Honesty involves behaving in a manner that is transparent. It is the responsibility of each person in the relationship to tell the truth and to be honest about the way they are feeling. The more time you spend together, the more comfortable you should be. If you feel as though you are uncomfortable sharing more personal information such as feelings with your partner, consider moving on as soon as possible so as not to give your partner a false sense of security.

Consideration. Consideration is a vital component in keeping any relationship alive. Being considerate involves being aware of your partner and making an effort to ensure they feel at ease physically and emotionally. Make a conscious effort not to be selfish by behaving in a way that outwardly demonstrates that you care. The best way to start is by using manners in your daily interactions with each other. This way you begin to form habits around making one another feel valued. Whether spoken or unspoken, there are certain rules that you should be aware of that if followed, will give any relationship the best possible chance of survival.

RELATIONSHIP DO'S AND DON'TS

- Do not lie about where you are going, where you have been or how you feel.
- Be aware of your partner's feelings and act accordingly.
- Be respectful of their opinions and where they may stem from.
- Compromise.
- Be thoughtful.
- Be demonstrative about your feelings.
- Don't be afraid to argue—arguments can help you better understand one another and are a healthy part of any relationship.
- Don't do anything that may hurt your partner's feelings such as making it aware that you find someone else attractive. It is normal to find other people attractive, but overtly making your partner feel inadequate is never okay.
- Don't abuse the other persons' trust in you in any way.

MEETING THE PARENTS

Being invited to meet your boyfriend's family is a big step in a relationship so it is important to make the best impression you can. Ultimately, you not only want them to approve their son's choice of partner, you want to leave them with the certainty that you are the best thing to have happened to their son since puberty. Even if the relationship ends eventually, making a good impression is still of utmost importance. You never know what may happen in the future so it is in your best interest to play by the rules. Bad impressions are like spots of rust on a gleaming reputation—don't take the risk.

What to Wear. You should look clean and tidy, so go for a polished feminine style that leans slightly toward conservative rather than 'wow'. Being thought of as well put-together involves some effort and styling but rest assured that it will all be worthwhile if his family think of you as the epitome of elegance. Don't go to any trouble trying to look like someone else either, just the best version of your 'ladies who lunch' self. Avoid showing too much skin, especially cleavage or upper thigh. This will get you nowhere and may significantly set you back in terms of convincing them of your excellent personality— the damage will have already have been done.

What to Bring. As any good guest knows, upon being invited to somebody's home, it is polite to bring a token of appreciation for the host. The same applies to meeting the family of your significant other. Ask your boyfriend about the sorts of things his mother would like in advance, she may be utterly obsessed with violets for instance. If your probing remains unsuccessful, offer to take dessert or some other such treat. Your efforts will be noticed and you will have made a good impression before you've even arrived.

How to Act. After the formal introductions, maintain open body language and make eye contact with everyone as you converse. Make an effort to speak with every family member individually over the course of your visit or risk being thought of as ill-mannered or standoffish. Avoid any overtly rude or personal anecdotes, crude language or voicing controversial opinions that may cause offense.

Instead, follow their conversational lead and contribute thoughtfully and enthusiastically where appropriate.

If a meal is served, ensure your table manners are impeccable and that you offer to help clear up. If they insist you remain seated, do so, knowing that your efforts will not have gone unnoticed. Use the words 'please' and 'thank you' liberally, and make a comment about the food being 'delicious' regardless of whether or not you think it is. Upon leaving comment on how lovely it was to meet everybody, thank them for having you.

EX-IQUETTE

When a relationship ends, you will either feel a sense of relief or sadness depending on the circumstances. While it is normal to feel a sense of loss and a myriad of other emotions, expect those feelings to subside as time passes and your life returns to normal. Regardless of if you are the dumpee or dumper, a breakup can be difficult for everyone involved. In order not to make matters worse, ensure you go about ending a relationship in a manner that is respectful and that aims to keep the dignity of the other person intact.

- Always end a relationship face to face rather than via telephone or text message. That would be cowardly and disrespectful.
- Never end a relationship by changing your relationship status on social media. Everyone deserves a truthful explanation.
- Do not begin a relationship until you have ended another.
- If the other person becomes emotional, do not become frustrated but be considerate of their feelings.
- Tell the truth about your reasons for wanting to break up, no

matter how hurtful. This enables the other person to move on and eliminates any chance for future heartache.

– Don't agree to 'stay friends' as this just prolongs the heartache. It also gives the other person a false sense of hope that there may be a chance for the relationship to be rekindled.

– Once ended, avoid all forms of contact such as phone calls and meeting for coffee 'to talk' for at least two months. This allows emotions to settle and prevents any irrational behavior.

– While it is your right to end a relationship if you so choose, it is also your responsibility to preserve the dignity of the other person when doing so.

BEING A GOOD FRIEND

Being loyal to your friends seems like an absolute no brainer. They're there for you when you are down, they support you in a crisis, they tell you how thin you still look when everybody knows you've put on weight and they let you borrow stuff from their wardrobe when the contents of yours simply won't do. Where your girlfriends are concerned, in order that they continue to do all of these things, you have to do them right back. That's how relationships of any kind work—they're about giving and taking and taking and giving. There is however, one exception to this rule, and that is, boys.

Friends and boys don't mix. Even if you have the world's biggest crush on a guy, if one of your friends has already admitted to the same crush out loud, you can never ever pursue, stalk, chat or flirt with the guy ever again. If you do, you are breaking the cardinal rule of friendship and can be guaranteed that a disaster will follow. Even if you have been in love with this boy since the moment he walked into your English class, even if you have thought about him every waking moment for the last two years, you can't do anything about it if a friend declares her crush aloud. That's just the way it goes.

Think about the consequences… whether you confess and reveal your years of torment or not, it will seem to everyone that you are just jealous and willing to sacrifice a friendship for a guy. It seems unfair but you must always remember that boys come and go a lot more rapidly that your true friends. So, if you have a crush, tell a couple of your friends as soon as you're sure and that way, they can vouch for you when another girl admits she likes the same guy. If you want to keep your group of friends and your reputation intact, never choose the short lived thrills and butterflies of a potential relationship over your friends because you'll end up eating a big, fat slice of everybody hates you pie, and washing it down with a nice, tall glass of diet lonely.

FRIENDSHIP DO'S AND DON'TS

- Listen. Everyone wants to be heard and at times, the best way to show support to a friend in need is by not saying a single word.
- Always take people as you find them. Never judge a person by the way they have been portrayed by others. Base your opinions solely on the way they treat you.
- Look out for each other's wellbeing.
  Make an effort to accept differences of opinion by understanding where those opinions come from.

- Treat friends with respect, as you would like to be treated.
- Never pursue the romantic interest of a friend. Avoid discussing, kissing, dating or becoming romantically involved with friends' boyfriends or ex-boyfriends. Even if you have permission, your friendship will eventually buckle under the tension.
- Make an effort on birthdays and in times of need. If you have made other plans, cancel and put your friend first.
- Do not engage or spread gossip about your friends, challenge anybody who does.

CHAPTER 11

SOCIAL MEDIA ETIQUETTE

"I fear the day that technology will surpass our human interaction.
The world will have a generation of idiots."
—Unknown

DIGITAL IMPRESSIONS

Using a social networking site like Facebook is a fantastic way to control the way people perceive you. You can create a montage of the most flattering photos to post to your profile and un-tag yourself in photos that make you look like King Kong. Great right? You can create an almost perfect version of yourself and change the image you're trying to convey with a simple click. It's the perfect supporting act to the festival of fabulousness you've got going on in the real world. Unfortunately, some people forget that and make terrible (sometimes horrific) mistakes that are difficult to erase from cyber space. To maintain your cool, you need to follow a few simple rules.

Firstly, watch your language. Being foul mouthed is not sexy or cool, so avoid any status updates that make you sound vulgar or cheap. Status updates are dangerous territory as it is. I mean really, does anybody care that you are drinking a latte at the beach? The answer is no. Avoiding simple status updates that make you appear as though you think the world is interested in your daily routine is a must. It's actually the same principle you would follow with a boy you fancy; be mysterious and people will naturally be drawn to you. There's nothing intriguing about telling the world via Facebook that you're having trouble deciding on the right outfit for a party.

Similarly, using slang is only ever acceptable if you are quoting someone for the purpose of making yourself seem hilarious. You can subtly make known how funny, alternative, intelligent, girly or eccentric you are, by choosing books, TV shows and movies that you like and displaying them in your profile. These things say a lot about you, so be yourself, choose wisely and be mindful that if your interests are 'boys,' your favorite TV show is 'Sex and the City' and your favorite quote is 'I'm too sexy for my…' then people will think you are an idiot or worse—a promiscuous idiot.

FACEBOOK DO'S AND DON'TS

—   Ensure you set your privacy setting to maximum security.
—   Do use Facebook to connect with friends and relatives at home and overseas.
—   Do use Facebook as means to open communication with long lost friends or acquaintances.
—   Share information that is humorous, informative, inspiring and inclusive.
—   Never use Facebook as a means of cyber bullying.
—   Always keep private information off Facebook including sensitive news such as a death in the family or a break-up. Tell those concerned personally.

- Do not accept friend requests from people you don't know.
- Do not post controversial opinions.
- Do not comment rudely on others' status updates.
- Do not post images or content that you wouldn't be comfortable showing a room full of strangers in real life.
- Do not post images or content that, in ten years from now, you wouldn't feel comfortable showing a room full of strangers in real life.
- Avoid posting selfies in an attempt to gain the approval of others. Excessive posting of selfies is indicative of insecurity.
- Avoid posting incriminating images or content of any kind.
- Avoid using Facebook as a soapbox from which to vent religious or political views or to insight racism or conflict.

INSTAGRAM ETIQUETTE

Instagram is a great way to share photos online but it isn't just an evolving digital photo album, it's a published representation of your identity. While you may be completely in control of the content you post, it's a good idea to be conscious of what that content says about you. Is your profile an online record of wonderful moments of your life that you capture and share with friends, or is it a series of selfies posted for the purpose of gaining acceptance from others? It's so easy to become caught up in the illusion that the number of 'likes' you receive reflects your worth as a person—it really doesn't at all. That is why it is important you take the time to nurture your relationships with friends and family and spend time working on being the best version of yourself in real life. Doing these things will give you a far greater sense of self-worth than any filtered picture can.

It is also important to learn how to be critical of the images you are consuming. Exposing yourself to hundreds of images of what other people think is beautiful can be dangerous if you haven't learned to love yourself as you are, especially if those images have been filtered. Often, photos of others that convey 'effortless perfection' have taken hours to capture and edit, and create an unrealistic sense of what beauty really is. True beauty comes from the inside after all.

The Technological Age has seen a dramatic shift in the whole idea of celebrity. Social media has created a space where we can view and interact with the celebrities we idolise online, creating the illusion that we are somehow taking part in their daily lives. Because platforms such as Instagram enable average people to emulate celebrity behavior, it becomes easy to believe that we are all celebrities in our own right, complete with our own 'fans' who 'follow' our every move. Without the assistance of an inner critic, it can become difficult to distinguish between the reality and the illusion. Ultimately, you should try to spend more time engaging in your real life so as to minimise the risk of being immersed in and subsequently drowned by the illusory one.

INSTAGRAM DO'S AND DON'TS

–   Don't become reliant on the number of likes you receive for a photo. This is in no way an indication of your worth as a human being.
–   Avoid trying to emulate celebrity behavior by posting selfies and videos that focus on appearance only. This can be perceived

as attention-seeking behavior and is a sign of low self-esteem.

- Never let your confidence be threatened when looking at pictures of others. You mustn't lose sight of the fact that most photos are edited and are therefore a false or unachievable representation of beauty.
- Never post negative comments on others' accounts. If you aren't contributing positively, avoid commenting all together.
- Never bully, harass or intimidate others online by posting negative comments on other peoples' content.
- Avoid excessive use of hashtags. This conveys a sense of desperation in terms of gaining likes or followers etc.
- Become critical of the content you are exposing yourself to. Ask yourself whether it is it having a positive or negative effect on your state of mind.
- Be mindful of the time you are spending consuming or reacting to other peoples' posts and increase your awareness of how you could be spending your time in a more productive way.
- Be considerate of others' experience of Instagram by limiting your posts to one or two per day.
- Ask yourself whether the images you are posting convey an attitude of superficiality before posting them.
- Practise being able to distinguish between advertisements and product endorsements, and neutral content.

SNAPCHAT ETIQUETTE

Snapchat can be a great way to share images and video content with friends. Unlike other photo sharing applications, the content disappears after a certain amount of time. This makes using the app. quite lifelike for the user because it mimics the process of a passing experience. Unfortunately, the fact that the content seems temporary, creates the illusion that the act of sending inappropriate material, be it sexually explicit or otherwise, has no serious consequences. However, just like other social networks like Facebook and Instagram, they have terms and conditions that enable them to use your content as they wish. Though it's absolutely not in their best interests to do so, always be aware that everything you publish online is being stored somewhere and at risk of being accessed by a third party. Always use common sense when it comes to using social networks; if you don't want your content to be saved and shared, don't post it.

SNAPCHAT DO'S AND DON'TS

- Avoid sending snaps that you wouldn't want others to save and share.
- Never take a screen shot of other peoples' content, the user will be alerted to the fact that someone has done so and it's generally considered unacceptable by Snapchat users.
- Don't publish photos or videos of others without their consent.
- Don't get seduced by the illusion that behaving like a celebrity will make you one. Posting a video of different angles of your face as you pout at the camera may be perceived as narcissistic behavior.

- Don't send images that are sexually explicit or contain nudity of any sort. Once you have sent an image, you have no control over its use and/or redistribution.
- Always send content that others may find interesting. Ten second snaps of your coffee will just be perceived as annoying.

TINDER ETIQUETTE

Meeting potential love interests on apps. such as Tinder has become popular for a number of reasons. The ease with which we can anonymously swipe through profiles and select people we deem to be attractive—without them even knowing—takes all the pressure out of dating. The swiping process in itself eliminates all the anxiety associated with the risk of rejection that occurs in real life interactions. We are collectively comforted by the fact that a person will only find out that we like them if the attraction is mutual. While this initial attraction may be purely based on looks and some general information, it is relatively easy to gain a good understanding of the kind of person your 'match' is and what their intentions are. For example, if a person is looking for a relationship, be it casual or otherwise, it should say so in their profile. If it doesn't, you can quickly find out in the 'chatting' phase. During this phase, clever questioning is a great way to establish whether or not the two of you may be compatible. Ultimately you are dealing with real people who have real feelings. Always be respectful and considerate in your interactions with others, be they online or otherwise.

TINDER DO'S AND DON'TS

- Ensure you have a range of profile pictures that convey the kind of person you are. Try to use photos that reflect your appearance in real life.
- Always include a short description of your interests and your intentions. This will enhance the overall image you have conveyed through your selection of photos.
- Ensure you use correct punctuation and grammar in your profile. The way you write speaks volumes about your character.
- Don't use provocative images as your profile pictures. This could lead to a misinterpretation of your intentions.
- Always keep your chat within the safety of the application until you feel comfortable. Giving away you phone number or any other personal details too quickly could put you in a potentially dangerous situation.
- Don't hesitate to use the 'unmatch' or 'report' functions if you feel uncomfortable or threatened in any way.
- Be observant while browsing. For example, if someone you find attractive appears drunk in every picture, a simple assumption can be made. Without casting judgement, if a person appears to be engaged in behavior that doesn't reflect the kind of person you are, swipe left.
- If a person clearly stipulates that they are only after a casual encounter, don't swipe right and hope that they will change their mind once they meet you. People have the right to their

own filtering process and respecting others in this way allows you to focus on finding someone with similar intentions.

– Be courteous by responding to messages as quickly as you can. Ignoring someone you have matched with may be perceived as rude and hurtful. If you are chatting with someone else, send a message saying that you are busy but that you will be in touch as soon as you can.

– Always speak with someone on the phone before you meet in real life. You can often tell a lot about a person by their tone of voice, the way they speak etc. If you feel as though you aren't compatible, politely end the conversation and use the 'unmatch' function.

– If you progress past the chatting phase and arrange to meet, always inform someone you trust of your whereabouts.

– If for whatever reason you don't feel a connection with the person you meet and they ask you out again, simply politely decline. Telling the truth about the way that you feel is always okay when prompted.

– Never use Tinder or any other dating app. while you are on a date.

– Once you have met in real life and a mutual attraction is confirmed, normal dating rules apply.

THE SELFIE

The worldwide popularity of the smartphone has given birth to the global phenomenon of the 'selfie'. For many people, taking pictures of themselves is appealing because of the complete control they have over their appearance. For others, it's a simple way of gathering pictorial evidence of the places they have been on their travels. Whatever the case, the humble selfie can reveal a lot about a person. The fact remains that a person's reputation is built upon how they are perceived by others, so gaining insight into the way selfies may be interpreted is very important if you want to maintain a good reputation.

Miss Self(ie)-Obsessed. Focusing on oneself with complete disregard for others is often interpreted as narcissistic behavior. That is, behavior that demonstrates an overwhelming need for admiration. It makes sense then, that taking and posting too many selfies, for whatever reason, lends itself to being labeled as such. When posting your personal photos on social media, make sure they reflect more about your life than merely superficial self-admiration. Being perceived as attractive by others involves far more than what appears on the surface. Don't use social media to create an artificial patchwork of pouty pictures, use it as a platform from which to convey the richness and complexity of your life—one that is more than skin-deep.

The 'Sexy Selfie'. Taking and posting provocative photos is a dangerous game, regardless of how good you or others think you appear in them. First of all, though self-confidence is a great quality to possess, posting revealing images can reveal much more than initially intended. Think about it, if all the photos you publish on social media are of your scantily clad self, it sends a clear message about your values. If you appear to value body image above all else, you may come across as shallow or insecure. Moreover, many girls fall into the trap of equating their self-worth with the number of 'likes' they receive on sites such as Facebook or Instagram. This can be catastrophic in terms of depleting your stores of self-esteem. Importantly, depending on your age, sending photographs of a sexually explicit nature to others is against the law. Sometimes, terrible mistakes come from ideas that 'seemed to be very good at the time' so always proceed with caution when it comes to taking sexy snaps.

CREATING A POSITIVE DIGITAL FOOTPRINT

Instant information is one of the luxuries of a technologically advanced world. At the touch of a button, personal information about you can be sourced online through social media platforms such as Facebook, Instagram and Twitter. Pictorial evidence of the sort of people you associate with and what you enjoy doing in your free time, can quickly add up to form a clear picture of the type of person you are. For this reason it is very important to proceed with caution when it comes to creating online profiles. It has become commonplace for employers to filter through extensive lists of potential employees by engaging in some online research first. If they come across anything (whether it be written information or images) that may question your character or suitability for a position, you will be struck off a shortlist faster than it took you to upload the photo in the first place.

As confident as you may be about the suitability of the information that you are putting online, know that as you mature, the things you like will change, including the image of yourself you wish to convey to the world. As easy and tempting as it may be to snap and post a photo of yourself being 'fabulous', be aware that what you consider 'fabulous' will differ substantially across generations and cultures. Use common sense and ask yourself whether the content you are publishing online is suitable for an audience that may include a potential employer. If you have to think twice about it, it's probably best not to share it on the World Wide Web. The good news is that you can still enjoy the benefits of social media by creating a positive online presence. All you need to do is follow a few simple steps. Use the following as a guide:

– Never post photos that depict illegal activities or your participation in them.
– Never post photos in which you appear intoxicated or under the influence of anything.
– Ensure you do not post any material that is provocative or indecent.
– Ensure that images of yourself that appear online convey attractive rather than antisocial behavior.
– Ensure all privacy settings are set to maximum security so that you can exercise some sort of control over how you share personal information.

BUILDING AND PROTECTING YOUR PERSONAL BRAND

If you must have a social presence online, you need to ensure your professional and social profiles are separate from one another. As such, no information pertaining to your social or personal life should be visible on a professional online profile. LinkedIn for example, is one of the biggest professional networks in the world. Often touted as 'Facebook for professionals' is a great networking tool for recent graduates aiming to expand their professional connections. However, one wrong move here and even the most pristine profile can become tainted.

When building a professional profile, simplicity and clarity are imperative in terms of the message you are putting out into the employment arena. Ensure you include information that is truthful and accurate, even if you don't necessarily think a position you have held in the past is in any way pertinent to your future employment aspirations. This is due to the fact that having a job is often held in higher regard than having no job at all. Also, if a potential employer can see that you have been promoted or have quickly risen through the ranks of any workplace, they will assume that you are enthusiastic and capable. As with any information made accessible to the public, avoid the inclusion of any material that may make you less attractive to potential employers. This includes the use of nicknames, in-jokes and crude comments.

SPRING CLEANING YOUR PROFILE

In good news, you can tidy up any accidental damage by ensuring all your security settings are set to maximum. Delete or 'untag' yourself from any images online that may invite negative interpretations of who you are. Be sure to filter your language too, taking care to present the best version of yourself to the world. The last thing you want are tacky or indecent images of yourself floating around online—they may pop up every now and then to remind you of how cautious you should have been.

RISKY BUSINESS—RECOGNIZING THE DANGERS

Online communities in their various forms can be relatively easy to navigate once you become comfortable with your interactions within them. But what are the limitations of such interactions? It is important to be aware of the dangers that lurk behind the prettiest of pictures on the internet. While technological communication offers a degree of anonymity, it may also create a sense of detachment from reality, thereby making it easier for people to say and do things that would be considered inappropriate in real life.

Let's use internet dating as an example. People have complete creative control over how they present themselves online, which in some cases, can lead to an overdeveloped sense of confidence.

If this confidence escalates out of control, it would be quite easy for a person become so absorbed in their online identity, that they begin to morph into an entirely different version of themselves! Posing as someone else online is deceitful and sometimes even dangerous, yet it is surprisingly common. Sexual predators have taken advantage of many an innocent victim by feigning familiarity, building trust and then luring them out of the safety of their homes. Think about how much personal information can be obtained about someone with the smallest amount of research. In the wrong hands this information could lead to disastrous consequences. That is why you need to take certain precautions regarding the sharing of information online. Think of the internet as a public place, be savvy and take care not to engage in risky behavior.

DIGITAL DO'S AND DON'TS

–   Do not accept friend requests from people if you do not share any mutual friends. You never know who may be behind the image or the 'kind' words on the screen.

–   Always keep your wits about you when chatting to people you don't know personally. Never give away any personal information including bank details, your home address, your school or place of work and always be aware that doing so is allowing a potential predator into the safety of your own home.

–   Do not distribute images of yourself that depict nudity or are sexual in nature. Once they are in cyberspace, you have absolutely no control over their use or redistribution. Similarly avoid any kind of 'sexting' even if you completely trust the intended recipient.

–   Never assume you are smarter than an online predator. They know what they are doing and are expert manipulators, often building trust and familiarity before you even realize what is happening.

–   Never use your camera to chat to a stranger online, again, by default you are letting them into the safety of your home, in some cases your bedroom. It is amazing what information can be gathered about a person from observing the contents of their room so be smart and keep your personal life exactly that— personal.

–   If someone online makes you feel uncomfortable, tell someone immediately. Never underestimate the power of instinct, even if it is just a hunch. Talk to someone, a friend or family member perhaps and let them know if you're finding it hard to disassociate with someone online.

– Seek help from family, friends or your doctor if you are struggling with various aspects of life as a young adult. Don't post images of yourself in harms' way or post anything that may allude to false attempts at suicide or self-harm. While behaving in this way will bring a lot of attention, it will be negative attention, which could serve to make matters worse.

– Never post material that may be culturally sensitive, offensive, racist or overtly opinionated. If you wish to express an opinion of that nature, find ways to do so outside the online community, express your feelings in a journal perhaps. Just remember that freedom of expression and intentional offence are not the same thing. Use your words wisely and you can use social media platforms to explore the world. The possibilities are endless!

CHAPTER 12

ANTI-SOCIAL BEHAVIOR

---

*"It is a wise thing to be polite; consequently, it is a stupid thing
to be rude. To make enemies by unnecessary and wilful incivility,
is just as insane a proceeding as to set your house on fire.
For politeness is like a counter—an avowedly false coin,
with which it is foolish to be stingy."*
—Arthur Schopenhauer

Anti-social behavior refers to any behavior that is not conducive to the collective needs of a community, or that fails to show consideration for others within that community. In other words, being selfish. The dangers of falling into the trap of being selfish are many but ultimately, it will be your reputation that suffers the consequences. You see, when people outwardly demonstrate behavior that conveys disrespect for other people, they are often perceived as ill-mannered or rude. If actions define a person and those actions are deemed as anti-social, then the consequences may cause irreparable damage reputation.

WHAT'S THE BIG DEAL?

If you wish to be successful, professionally or otherwise, you need to stand out for the right reasons rather than the wrong ones. One of the most significant features of contemporary Western Culture is our obsession with instant gratification. Everything is instant. Unfortunately, one of the side effects of growing up in a world where you can have anything you want, as soon as you want it, is an attitude commonly referred to as 'a sense of entitlement'. So what does a sense of entitlement look like? Well, it's an outlook that's self-centered and inwardly focused. For example, a person with a sense of entitlement has a 'what's in this for me' attitude. When you project this attitude to others, it sends out an air of selfishness—the opposite of the qualities of positive, attractive behavior that have been described in this book.

BULLYING

Bullying is the personification of anti-social conduct. It occurs when there is a repeated attempt to harm or intimidate another person. It happens at schools, in workplaces and thanks to social media, in the bedrooms of innocent victims everywhere. When someone acts in a manner that completely fails to recognize the feelings of another human being, bonds begin to weaken and relationships begin to corrode. As such, it is vital that we reflect on our actions and constantly strive to be better at being aware of others. Use the information below to identify the various types of bullying so that you can play your role in stopping it.

Physical. Physical bullying occurs when a person is subjected to regular, targeted harassment by an individual or group. It is confronting and aggressive and can involve pushing, shoving, slapping and physical threats. It may also be sexual in nature.

Emotional. Emotional bullying is the repeated intention to hurt or humiliate a person through name calling or mocking, belittling, tormenting and excluding conduct. A person being bullied in this way may not have any signs of physical harm but may display other signs such as a change in demeanor, loss of confidence and depression.

Cyber. Cyber bullying is any kind of bullying that occurs through the use of technology. It is one of the most devastating forms of bullying as it can be difficult to escape, it is visible to so many people and difficult to remove once online.

BULLYING DO'S AND DON'TS

- Don't bully anybody, ever.
- Be polite and practice good manners wherever you go.
- Seek support from parents, teachers, counselors or family friends if you or anybody you know is being bullied.
- Don't be a bystander. Bullying is unacceptable, say so.
- Offer support to friends in need by listening to their concerns.
- Help them seek support if you feel ill equipped to deal with it.
- Never use the anonymity of being online as an excuse to bully someone.

- Don't go out of your way to intimidate, threaten or hurt someone else.
- If anybody you know speaks about self-harming or suicide (including posting images online that relate to such things), alert someone immediately.
- If you feel as though you are being harassed online, don't respond. Log off immediately and talk to someone you trust.
- Avoid using technology in your bedroom. Reserve your room as a safe haven where you can take the time to relax.
- Keep a record of any nasty comments, images, messages or threats you may be receiving and report the bullying immediately.

FAUX PAS

Faux pas is a French term meaning 'false step' and it is used to describe instances of tactless or embarrassing conduct. If you do make an unintentional faux pas, the best thing to do is excuse yourself, apologize if appropriate and continue as you were before the slip up.

Looking at Your Mobile Phone. Talking, texting, tweeting, playing games, using social media and anything else that can be done on a phone is unacceptable in the company of others. Be aware of the fact that whenever you are on your phone, it is an outward display of where your priorities lie. Whether you are in a social, professional or academic setting, do not use your phone if:

A) you are being addressed by another
B) your attention is required.

Not only is it considered poor conduct, you may be distracted to the point where the safety of other people is compromised.

Rude Phone Use	Dangerous Phone Use
In conversation	Driving or operating machinery
At the table, dining, eating	Walking
During a meeting or presentation	Cycling
When you should be working, assisting, serving or attending to others	Crossing a road
While at a party, or formal occasion	While boarding and alighting transport
When others are socializing	Onboard airplanes
While in a shop	While walking alone at night
While in a medical center, bank or library where a quite ambience is required	

Taking Food into a Café or Restaurant. Never take your own food or drink into an establishment whose business is based around providing food and drink. Using the tables and chairs of a café to consume food you have obtained elsewhere is unacceptable. For example, leaving a restaurant and coming back moments later with an ice cream shows complete disregard for those that run the business.

Failure to Make Eye Contact. One of the most common faux pas is the inability to make eye contact with all people involved in a group discussion. The irony here is that while most people will feel excluded from the conversation, the culprit probably lacks confidence. For whatever reason, when speaking to a group, always make eye contact with everyone involved.

Inappropriate Touching. Inappropriate touching and other such invasions of personal space happen quite frequently and often go unchecked. If someone touches you in any way that makes you feel uncomfortable, politely tell them to stop. Never pat anybody on the head, stroke or touch any part of a person's body unless you are rescuing them from harm, offering support or involved in an established relationship.

Commenting on Others Appearance. If you aren't planning on saying anything nice, then it probably remains best unsaid. This includes backhanded compliments and unwelcome statements about a person's appearance. For instance, never exclaim something like 'oh, you've changed your hairstyle' unless you are going to follow with a compliment such as, 'it looks lovely'. As a general rule, think before speaking and don't make comments that are open to interpretation.

Failure to Accept Compliments. When someone goes out of their way to give you a compliment, it is considered polite to say thank you. Many people think that accepting a compliment may make them appear conceited when in fact, the opposite is true.

Yawning or Stretching. Whether you are being addressed in person or as a part of a group, it is important to listen with your ears as well as your body. Yawning or stretching while someone else is speaking is extremely bad manners. It sends the message that you do not want to be there and that you are not in any way interested in the information being presented. If unsure when this rule may apply, imagine how you would feel in a similar situation and adjust your body language accordingly.

Failure to Introduce People. If someone approaches you and you are in company, it is common courtesy to introduce that person in order to make them feel at ease. If you are with an impossibly large group of people, break away from them slightly to avoid any awkwardness.

The Correct Way to Walk into a Room. When entering a space in which others are already engaged in some kind of activity, presentation or discussion, never walk across the room or in front of anybody who may be speaking. Always remain at the entrance until you have made eye contact with the appropriate person before quietly finding the closest seat. If you are late, mouth the word 'sorry' to acknowledge your tardiness and try to cause as little disruption as possible as you take your seat.

Name Dropping. Nobody likes a namedropper. Avoid boasting about people you know that may be wealthy or have some sort of celebrity status. This will make you appear pretentious and shallow.

Talking About Money. Whether you are dripping in money or drowning in debt, be discreet about it. Speaking about your financial woes makes others feel uncomfortable and awkward, and bragging about wealth elicits the same response.

In conversations, professional or otherwise, it is considered uncouth to ask anybody how much money they have, earn or are entitled to. Try to project values that aren't based around material things, such as truth, friendship, honesty and love.

Over-sharing. Never feel that you have to vocalize all of your thoughts. Take using the bathroom for example, never relay 'bathroom experiences' (or any other such anecdotes for that matter) to friends or colleagues because, at the end of the day, nobody wants to know. Assuming everybody has the same level of intestinal fortitude as yourself is a common mistake. Be satisfied in the knowledge that some things are just better left unsaid.

CHAPTER 13

TRANSITIONING INTO ADULTHOOD

*"There is nothing noble about being superior to some other man.
The true nobility is in being superior to your previous self."*
—Hindu Proverb

Life is full of hurdles, some little and some big, and we spend most of our time trying to get over, under, around and even through them. Whatever the case, the more hurdles we pass, the stronger we become. As our character begins to grow and develop in this way, we become more resilient, more able to cope with the exhaustion of trying to jump the hurdles. Use the following information as a guide to help you find your way around the obstacle course of becoming a responsible adult.

SHARED ACCOMMODATION ETIQUETTE

"Practice yourself in little things… and thence proceed to greater."
—Epictetus

Living away from home can be a wonderful experience and is often a young adult's first real taste of freedom and independence. As with anything though, with freedom and independence comes great responsibility, the most significant of course being responsibility for oneself. Living with other people not only reinforces the importance of personal responsibility, it teaches us how to be tolerant of others' beliefs and considerate of their feelings. The following guide will help you navigate your way through the often unreliable terrain of living with other people.

Cleaning. Cleaning up after yourself is important whether you live alone or in shared accommodation. It is vital that you engage in two types of cleaning, the major type of cleaning that should happen once a week and the minor cleaning that happens on a daily basis for upkeep.

– Bathroom. Once a week, the bathroom should be thoroughly cleaned. This includes the inside of the toilet, the shower, taps, glass surfaces, windows, mirrors and the floor. Use rubber gloves, hot water and a suitable cleaning agent. Ensure the cleaning equipment you use in the bathroom is not used anywhere else.

– Kitchen. Once a week, the kitchen needs the same attention. This includes all surfaces including the floor, the stovetop, sink, the inside of the oven and the microwave. Do dispose of any items in the refrigerator that may have spoiled or passed their use by date and clean up any miscellaneous spills whose remnants may be lurking in the dark recesses of the middle shelf. This will prevent any unidentifiable bacteria from growing between cleans. Between weekly cleans, focus on the basics such as cleaning up after preparing a meal, wiping bench tops etc.

– Communal Areas. Communal areas need to be vacuumed and dusted once a week and any glass surfaces such as tabletops and windows need to be polished.

Rosters. So who will be doing all this cleaning? As soon as you move in, a roster should be created for the fair and even distribution of household chores. Role descriptions should be clearly marked, expectations should be clarified in terms of quality control and measures should be put into place in the event that someone cannot complete their fair share of the workload. As the saying goes, many hands make light work, if the roster is agreed upon by all, cleaning up will be a breeze.

Communal vs Personal Space. Avoid placing personal items in a communal space. It is likely that that tastes among flatmates will vary considerably so don't assume anyone would like to pass their time gazing adoringly at your life-size Mickey Mouse lamp. Imposing your tastes onto others is never okay. Agreeing to keep communal areas neutral is the easiest option for everybody involved.

Rent and Bills. It is your responsibility to pay all your rent and bills on time. Keep abreast of what you owe and to whom and never 'dip' into the miscellaneous money jar for 'necessities' such as pizza. If you cannot afford to pay the rent, move somewhere more affordable. It is never acceptable to be a financial burden on your flatmates.

Dinner. Establish a routine, whatever it is, and stick to it. Whether it's a dinner roster, or every man for themselves, establishing a dinner routine is crucial for the smooth running of any household. Committing to dinner with your flatmates and forgetting about it can be extremely frustrating for the person whose job it was to prepare the meal, so be considerate of others at all times.

Meetings. Have regular meetings to discuss any issues or resolve any conflicts that may have arisen. Leaving tension to build up is not advisable and may lead to awkwardness or animosity between flatmates.

Guests. Do arrive at a consensus when it comes to guests. If you have to, establish visiting hours that suit everybody's needs. If people are constantly dropping in and out, it can be quite frustrating for any flatmate trying to escape the hustle and bustle of a stressful work life. Remember, a home is a sanctuary so be mindful of disturbing the peace.

Parties. If you want to have a party, whether it's a formal dinner party or 50 people dancing on your balcony, you need to be prepared. Let your neighbors know in advance and assure them that any noise your guests are making will cease at a certain time. Whatever time you select, stick to it. This will ensure you gain their respect and heighten your chances of being able to host more parties in the future. If you have the support of your flatmates to go ahead, remember to clean up the mess in the morning.

Privacy. Being aware of peoples' varying levels of tolerance comes in handy when it comes to shared accommodation. Never assume your flatmates wish to see you in your underwear or your birthday suit. Be discreet and save everybody the possible embarrassment of having to tell you to cover up. Do not expect to be left alone if you are seated in a communal area, if you wish to be left alone for whatever reason, retire to your bedroom and close the door. Never barge into someone else's room without knocking first and only open the door if you clearly hear the words 'come in'. Knocking once before barging in is rude and defeats the purpose of knocking.

Trouble in Paradise. The likelihood that you will disagree with one or all of your flatmates at some time or other is quite high. Expect tensions to rise, emotions to gush and tempers to flare. When this happens, keep calm. Being upset is completely acceptable, being rude or aggressive on the other hand, is not. Calmly try to resolve the issue by respectfully discussing the matter. This means that you need to actively listen to the concerns of the other person. If anybody concerned becomes too emotional for a discussion to take place, suggest cooling down before revisiting the issue the following day. Always treat your flatmates with dignity. Accept responsibility for the way your actions may have affected them and apologize if necessary. Expect the same in return.

ACADEMIC ETIQUETTE

"Each of us must work for his own improvement, and at the same time share a general responsibility for all humanity."
—Marie Curie

Wherever the classroom, be it school, college or university, your success and the success of others will depend on mutual respect and the quality of the learning environment. Understanding the fundamentals of etiquette will help you reach your potential by enabling you to create the conditions required for an optimal learning experience.

Two Sides, One Coin. If you maintain that you have the right to a quiet learning environment, you must also maintain the responsibility to do your part in creating one. If you wish to be heard, speak up and if you wish to achieve, work hard. If you wish to be treated with humility and respect, you must make a priority of treating others the same way. If you wish to progress you must push forward and if you wish to succeed, you must do all that is within your power to try.

Preparation. Don't be left behind by failing to complete work or bring equipment. Catching up is difficult if you have fallen behind. Not only are you doing yourself a disservice by being unprepared, you are impacting on the learning of others who may have to wait for you to catch up.

Questions. Never be afraid to ask questions. Thoughtful questions promote discussion and discussion is a fundamental element of the learning process. Each time a question sparks a discussion, you are moving forward.

Commitment. Making a commitment to finish what you start, although difficult, is the fastest way to reaping the rewards of academic achievement in any classroom. If you are present in body, be present in mind.

Curiosity. Be curious. Ask questions. Make sure you get the most out of the learning environment and the expertise of the person leading the learning. Never assume you already know it all, as is most often the case, the more we learn, the more we discover how little we know.

Standards. Set high standards for yourself. If you think you can do better, you know you can do better. Expect the best and push yourself until you are producing the best quality work possible. The more you expect of yourself, the closer you will be to achieving your goals.

Group Work. Most people cringe at the thought of having to complete a task outside of the classroom with a group of strangers. The inconvenience of having to organize a meeting place, ensuring work has been distributed fairly, let alone trying to establish who will complete which part of the task. The list goes on. However inconvenient though, group tasks are excellent training for the workplace. They encourage teamwork, highlighting its importance in everyday life as well as within professional environments.

Teamwork teaches lessons about compromise and allows students to deal with the various needs and wants of different personalities in the learning environment.

While these are just some of the benefits of collaborative learning, to get the most out of it, one needs to ensure they take responsibility for their role within the group. Students should arrive on time to meeting places, be prepared in terms of work completed and equipment, be cooperative, considerate and tolerant of others. Students that fail to comply with these basic requirements risk losing credibility and in turn, developing a bad reputation.

ACADEMIC WORLD DO'S AND DON'TS

- Do turn off phones and other electronic devices that may distract you or other students.
- Don't make excuses.
- Take responsibility.
- Respect others' right to a quiet learning environment.
- Avoid interrupting people when they are speaking.
- Respect the opinions of others, even if you disagree with them.
- Have an open mind, intellectual arrogance is often interpreted as ignorance.
- Be prepared. Failure to complete your share of work shows disregard for the efforts of others.
- Be punctual.
- Be polite.
- Be respectful of the teacher/presenter/facilitator.
- Raise your hand to speak.

– Don't dominate question time or bombard the class with endless irrelevant comments or personal anecdotes.

HOUSE GUEST ETIQUETTE

*"Kindness is a language which the deaf can hear
and the blind can see."*
—Mark Twain

When invited to stay with someone for an extended period of time, there are certain guidelines that need to be followed out of respect for the person who has welcomed you into their home. By doing this, they have gone out of their way to do you a favor, not the other way around. Taking your time to familiarize yourself with the following guidelines will ensure you are considered 'the perfect house guest' wherever you go.

Organization. Be sure to have everything under control in terms of arrival times and transport. Where you can, try not to inconvenience your host by asking extra favors of them such as collecting you from the train station or airport. Exercise independence here, your host will appreciate your efforts. They have already gone out of their way to have you in their home, so out of respect it is very important you demonstrate how thankful you are without unnecessarily interrupting their daily life any more than you already have.

Adapting to Change. When staying in someone's home, their rules apply. For some people this may require a change in routine. For instance, you may not tend to go to sleep until midnight but if your host has children, it may be the case that the household generally tends to be in bed by 9pm. In this case, it would be appropriate to wind down when they do, causing minimal noise and disruption.

Perfect Timing. Observe the daily routine of your host. If there seems to be a peak period of bathroom traffic between the hours of 7am and 8am, it would be inappropriate of you to try to shower during this time. Remember, it is not your home, you need to demonstrate an attitude that says 'your daily routine takes priority over mine'.

Helping Hand. Assisting with general chores and the daily upkeep of your host's home is absolutely necessary. It shows them that you are thankful for the effort they have gone to making your life easier. Be observant, offer to help with cooking, cleaning, washing and ironing. Always wash and iron your own clothes. If you have your own room, keep it clean and tidy and make your bed every day without fail. If you are sleeping in a communal area, pack your bed away every day so that the area can be used throughout the day as it normally would be.

Disappearing Acts of Kindness. Knowing when it is appropriate to 'disappear' is crucial. Everybody needs their privacy and being able to sense your host's need for it could make or break your reputation as a heavenly house guest. If your host is having a heated argument with someone on the phone, likewise if they are discussing personal family business, you should take it upon yourself to leave the room. Actively demonstrate that you are giving them privacy. Similarly, if a disagreement breaks out after dinner between the friends of family members of your host, do not voice your opinion. Just because you are there, does not mean that you are invited to share your views on the matter. In some cases, it may be appropriate to either leave the room or go for a walk. Whatever the case, giving your host 'space' to air their grievances in private will be a welcome gesture.

Contributing. As a guest, it is likely that you will have been invited to share food and meals with your host. If this is the case, offering to contribute to the cost of the groceries and anything else you see fit is absolutely appropriate. Every time your host spends money, if you are indirectly benefiting from the purchase, it is your duty to contribute. If this becomes awkward or stressful, simply insist that you contribute a weekly amount and leave it at that. You may also like to treat your host to a meal or two, depending on the length of your stay, to show your appreciation.

Independence. Never assume it is appropriate to tag along with your host wherever they go. Ensure family outings remain as such by making your own arrangements. Be respectful by making them aware of your plans and by all means leave notes with information pertaining to your daily schedule and what time they should expect your return. This shows that you are actively trying to minimize any impact your being in their home could have.

Respect. Respect the home of your host and everything within it. If you use something, put it back where you got it from, if you spill something, clean it up and if you break something, apologize profusely and offer to replace it. If you are not a child under ten, these rules apply.

Pleasantries. Be polite and well mannered. Smile often and say 'please' and 'thank you' liberally. Demonstrate impeccable table manners and dining etiquette, informal or otherwise, and make an effort to adapt your behavior to whatever is deemed suitable by your host. Always aim to ensure others feel at ease in your company by going out of your way to show gratitude.

BABY SHOWER AND BRIDAL KITCHEN TEA ETIQUETTE

"Their manners are more gentle, kind,
than of our generation you shall find."
—William Shakespeare, The Tempest

Attending baby showers and bridal kitchen teas can be a lot of fun if everybody plays by the rules. Whether in a garden, a park or someone's home, these events are all about the mothers and brides to be. Although it has become a common practice to have a gift registry for these events, it is never inappropriate to select your own thoughtful gift instead. Historically, the registry has been used as a strategy to prevent being given fifty of the same gift, so if you do opt out, be sure to put some thought into the gift.

Presents! Contrary to popular belief it is up to the guest of honor to decide whether or not to open the gifts in front of the other guests.

There are two schools of thought here, the first being that it is polite to facilitate a public festival of gratitude, and the second is that the process should occur privately in order that no guest feels as though their gift is inadequate. Whichever way the gifts are opened, thank you cards should be sent. If you are a close friend of the bride or mother to be and the presents are opened then and there, offer to make a written record of the gifts and who brought them. This makes the process of writing thank you cards is as easy as possible for the guest of honor over the following week.

DRIVING ETIQUETTE

When using the road with other motorists it is necessary to follow the road rules responsibly and to exercise caution at all times. If you wish to feel safe on the road then the first thing you need to do is drive in a manner that does not put anybody else in danger. It really is as simple as that. The fundamental principles of etiquette primarily involve being considerate of others so next time you get behind the wheel, be considerate in your quest to avoid the following driving faux pas.

Merging, Merging! Failure to let people merge in traffic is a big no, no. Not only is it inconsiderate and rude, it disrupts the flow of motorists trying to get to their respective destinations. If an entire lane of traffic needs to merge, it is important that they are let in one car at a time. For this process to work effectively, each car in the steady lane must be responsible for letting a vehicle in from the merging lane. This is considered common courtesy.

Get Off the Phone. It is against the law to use your mobile phone while driving. Moreover, it is irresponsible and dangerous. A driver needs to be focused on the road at all times, not to mention looking out for any other motorists, pedestrians, cyclists and anything else that may be a potential hazard. It only takes a split second for a collision to occur so be vigilant when it comes to resisting the urge to text or chat. If being on your phone is second nature, place it on the back seat so that it remains out of your reach for the entire journey. If you are a passenger and the driver is using their phone, it is acceptable to politely ask them to put it down. If they are well-mannered, they should be happy to make you feel at ease in their company.

Double Parking. It is never acceptable to block the vehicle of another person. You can never predict other people's circumstances, nor assume that you will be back before they are. If you need to stop momentarily, avoid being selfish and walk an extra block if you have to. 'Parking people in' causes traffic to build up and may block the view of oncoming traffic for pedestrians—a dangerous combination of potential hazards to say the least.

Mobile Disco. Turn your music down at traffic lights if it is loud enough to be heard from outside of the car. Be considerate of others who may not necessarily appreciate the same kind of music as you do. Just as you need to concentrate on the road, so do other motorists so be aware of what you are doing and how it may impact on the driving experience of others.

Road Rage. Violent and intimidating behavior is unacceptable inside a car and out. If a fellow motorist makes a mistake or even behaves dangerously, there is always a better way to express your concern than by throwing a violent tantrum. Being well mannered also involves being able to deal with people that aren't, so remain calm and take a mental note of the offenders' license plate. If you still think their behavior on the road warrants affirmative action, call the police and report the incident. If you are on the receiving end of road rage, do not react in any way other than an initial gesture of apology. If the behavior becomes increasingly intimidating, drive to the nearest police station.

Get Off My Back! Tailgating is intimidating for the driver in front as it puts them under a significant amount of pressure to speed up. If you are rushing, avoid tailgating at all costs. The person in front may have to stop suddenly in which case you could drive directly into the back of their car. Conversely, if you are being tailgated, ensure you move to the slow lane to let the culprit pass. If this is impossible, continue to drive at the speed limit until you reach your destination.

Thank You. Whenever anybody makes your driving experience easier by exhibiting patience, allowing you to merge or letting you pass, say thank you by waving your hand in front of the rear mirror. Failure to do so is the height of rudeness and one of the most loathed of all driving faux pas.

Disabled Parking. Never park in a reserved space, especially if it is marked 'Disabled Parking Only'. Not only is frowned upon to park in spaces that are reserved for people that have a disability, it is unkind.

PEDESTRIAN ETIQUETTE

Being a pedestrian can be dangerous. With this in mind, it is essential that you understand the specific conduct associated with sensible walking. Motorists have a difficult job as it is, don't risk your safety or the safety of others by failing to be a responsible pedestrian.

Keep Left, or Right! When using a footpath, it's important to stick to one side in order to promote the safety, comfort and easy flow of other pedestrians. If you aren't sure which side you should be walking on, use the traffic as a guide. If the cars driving in the same direction as you walking are on the left, stick to the left, and vice versa.

Step Aside! Remaining alert in busy areas is a must when trying to navigate your way through crowds on foot. If you are walking in a group, be sure to break up and allow people opposite you to pass. Failure to do so could be perceived as rude or intimidating and may put the other pedestrian in harm's way if they are pushed onto the street, for example.

Pay Attention. Do not text, tweet, email or anything else on your phone while walking. This causes congestion on paths where the smooth flow of traffic depends on the conscious effort of everyone to play by the rules.

Yikes! Bikes. If you wish to ride a bike, do so on designated bike tracks or paths. Never ride a bike on a footpath. If you are using the road, make sure you follow the road rules judiciously and above all wear a helmet at all times. When passing pedestrians, lightly ring the bell once to alert them that you are passing by. This gesture is not only polite but may prevent sudden movements that could result in an accident.

Dawdling. At a crossing, a pedestrian has an exclusive right of way when the signal shows it is their turn to cross the road. However, if crossing a section of road without signals, do stop and look before attempting to cross. Adopt a sense of urgency where you can, walking slowly across the road where there are no lights is not only dangerous, but extremely rude.

Hands Off. Never lean on a car that is not yours out of respect for the property of other people. It is considered bad manners. Regardless of whether you are wearing an item of clothing that may scratch the paintwork, the car is not yours to lean on.

SPORTSMANSHIP

*"Victory is in the quality of the competition
and not the final score."*
—*Mike Marshall*

Being a 'good sport' is a life skill, high on list of qualities that people value most. Whatever the game, the ability to be gracious in victory or defeat takes time to master. When playing sport, either professionally or socially, adopting the following practices will set you in the right direction:

- Learn the rules—all of them.
- Don't cheat.
- Acknowledge your mistakes.
- If you injure a teammate or opponent make sure they are okay and help them up if possible.
- Be mindful of your language. Do not swear.
- Always be respectful of the decisions of the officials.
- Shake hands (with sincerity) with your opponent regardless of whether you won or lost.
- Attend all training sessions to avoid letting your teammates down.
- Remain in control of your emotions whether you win or lose. Never throw a tantrum when things do not go to plan.
- Never cheer an opponent's error.
- Respect sporting equipment.

CHAPTER 14

LADIES AND GENTLEMEN

*"It's a funny thing about life, if you refuse to accept
anything but the best, you very often get it."*
—Somerset Maugham

By definition, the word *ladylike* refers to the embodiment of qualities such as refinement, grace and sophistication while the word *gentleman* connotes honor, chivalry and courtesy. The wonderful thing about acting in a manner that is considered ladylike or gentlemanly, is that it attracts ladies and gentlemen. Even more than that, it makes you seem approachable, attractive and warm. So what do gentlemen look like exactly? How old are they? Where do they hide? Rest assured, they come in all ages, shapes and sizes, from all walks of life. Here are a few telltale signs that your man is a true gent:

WHAT TO EXPECT FROM A GENTLEMAN

A true gentleman possesses qualities that surpass mere politeness. He exudes courtesy, putting the needs of others ahead of his own in a manner that says 'I genuinely care about other people'. He is quietly confident without being arrogant, strong but not aggressive and though humble in nature, he unconsciously commands the attention of others around him. A man of action, expect a gentleman to do the things he says he will, as well as those he does not mention. He will lead the way when you need him to, treat you with respect and honor your dignity.

Presentation is of utmost importance to a gentleman. Regardless of the price tag, his clothing will be neat and tidy and he will be immaculately groomed from head to toe. He will not raise his voice in public, nor will he cause an argument or make you feel embarrassed. A gentlemen always takes care of others and in his company, your needs will be his priority. Gentlemen make people feel at ease.

On a date, a gentleman will insist on paying the bill, especially on the first date. In a restaurant he will not start eating until you have, nor will he be distracted by anything—yes, including his phone. When you leave, he will insist that he accompany you to your car or walk you home and he will not make you feel obliged to do anything but say goodbye. If it's cold he will offer you his coat and if it's warm, he will offer to take yours. A gentleman will walk on the side of the footpath closest to the road and encourage you to go ahead of him through doorways that are always open.

A gentleman doesn't speak badly about others and is respected by his friends and colleagues. No matter his age or occupation, whatever he does, he does it well.

SHE'S A LADY

"Elegance is the only beauty that never fades."
—Audrey Hepburn

Yes, being ladylike means to be imbued with qualities such as style, sophistication, elegance, grace and courtesy, but being a lady is far more. It's something about the way that others feel when they're around her, they feel completely at ease. A lady is warm and friendly. Her kind nature is visible to most and she is comfortable in her own skin. Often putting the needs of others before her own, a lady always tries to be the best version of herself. She expects the very best, valuing quality over quantity and strives for a kind of personal success that is self-defined.

A lady has high expectations of others, paralleled only by those she places on herself. She is sensitive to others' feelings and discusses ideas rather than people. Never petty or rude, her manners are impeccable. Confident and humble, a lady feels comfortable in any social setting. She illuminates a crowd. Her social skills are finely tuned and she is ever prepared for the global stage.

On a date, a lady will offer to contribute to the bill, even though she knows that her date will insist otherwise. In a restaurant she will not start eating before others, nor will she be distracted by anything—yes, including her phone. A lady will notice everything, especially kind gestures and will never be vulgar or distasteful. She will let a gentleman walk her home or to her car but she won't invite him inside on a first date.

A lady does not succumb to peer pressure, or apply it. She is highly respected by her friends and colleagues. No matter her age or occupation, whatever she does, a lady does it well.

BEING A LADY DO'S AND DON'TS

– Be well-mannered.
– Always stand up straight and be aware of your posture.
– Endeavour to appear clean, neat and tidy at all times.
– Find a signature scent by selecting a perfume that suits your skin and wearing it every day.
– When sitting, ensure knees are together at all times and ankles are crossed. Nobody should ever be able to see or catch a glimpse of your underwear. If you are crossing your legs, be mindful of the amount of thigh showing.
– Never speak out of turn.
– Never use crude or inappropriate language.
– Adapt your speech and behavior to your environment.
– Avoid gossiping about others' personal affairs.
– Remain in control, never shout at anybody or throw a tantrum.
– Be mindful of others' feelings.
– Avoid trying to look provocative by showing too much skin.

SOURCES

page 10

Etiquette: The customary code of polite behavior in society or among members of a particular profession or group.
Definition of 'etiquette' from Oxford Dictionaries
Oxforddictionaries.com 23rd February 2015

page 13

"I have come to believe that our innate purpose is nothing more than to be the greatest version of ourselves. It is a process of refinement, improvement and enhancement. When you are aligned with this process and living your purpose, you have the potential of creating something amazing."
Dr. Steve Maraboli
Unapologetically You: Reflections on Life and the Human Experience
Goodreads.com 23rd February 2015

page 14

"The shortest and surest way to live with honor in the world, is to be in reality what we would appear to be; all human virtues increase and strengthen themselves by the practice and experience of them."
Socrates
The Forbes Book of Business Quotations: 14266 Thoughts on the Business of Life
Angelfire.com 23rd February 2015

page 14
"Good manners will open doors that the best education cannot."
Clarence Thomas
Goodreads.com 23rd February 2015

page 17
"...I tend to make up my mind about people within thirty seconds of meeting them... I rely far more on gut instinct than researching huge amounts of statistics."
Richard Branson
Losing My Virginity: How I've Survived, Had Fun and Made a Fortune Doing Business My Way
Goodreads.com 23rd February 2015

page 24
"The way to gain a good reputation is to endeavor to be what you desire to appear."
Socrates
Thinkexist.com 23rd February 2015

page 26
"Kindness in words creates confidence. Kindness in thinking creates profoundness. Kindness in giving creates love."
Lao Tzu
Thinkexist.com 23rd February 2015

page 27

"All our dreams can come true, if we have the courage to pursue them."
Walt Disney
Goodreads.com 28th May 2015

page 35

"If you have great talents, industry will improve them; if moderate abilities, industry will supply their deficiencies. Nothing is denied to well-directed labor: nothing is ever to be attained without it."
Sir Joshua Reynolds
The Works of Sir Joshua Reynolds, Volume 1
Books.google.com.au 23rd February 2015

page 38

"When I got here… they thought I worked 100 hours a day. Now, no matter what time I get in, nobody questions my ability to get the job done. Get it through your head, first impressions last. You start behind the eight ball, you'll never get in front."
Harvey Specter (character from *Suits*)
Imdb.com 23rd February 2015

page 40

"You cannot dream yourself into a character; you must hammer and forge yourself one."
Henry David Thoreau
Personalexcellence.com 23rd February 2015

page 42

"A customer is the most important visitor on our premises. He is not dependent on us. We are dependent on him. He is not an interruption on our work. He is the purpose of it. He is not an outsider on our business. He is a part of it. We are not doing him a favor by serving him. He is doing us a favor by giving us an opportunity to do so."

Kenneth B. Elliott

CTS Service Solutions

Customersthatstick.com 23rd February 2015

page 47

"The height of sophistication is simplicity."

Clare Boothe Luce

Quoteinvestigator.com 23rd February 2015

page 53

"For beautiful eyes, look for the good in others; for beautiful lips, speak only words of kindness; and for poise, walk with the knowledge you are never alone."

Sam Levenson

Goodreads.com 23rd February 2015

page 57

"Circumspection in calamity; mercy in greatness; good speeches in assemblies; fortitude in adversity: these are the self-attained perfections of great souls."

Hitopadesha

Great Thought Treasury

Greatthoughtstreasury.com 23rd February 2015

page 59

"The Art of Conversation: A certain self-control which now holds the subject, now lets it go with a respect for the emergencies of the moment."
Ralph Waldo Emerson
On Leaving: A Reading in Emerson Books.google.com.au 23rd February 2015

page 68

"In this life, when you deny someone an apology, you will remember it at a time when you beg forgiveness."
Toba Beta
My Ancestor was an Ancient Astronaut
Goodreads.com 23rd February 2015

page 77

"Do your little bit of good where you are; it's those little bits of good put together that overwhelm the world."
Desmond Tutu
The Desmond Tutu Peace Foundation
Tutufoundation-usa.org 23rd February 2015

page 87

"For to be free is not merely to cast off one's chains, but to live in a way that respects and enhances the freedom of others."
Nelson Mandela
The Independent

Independent.co.uk 23rd February 2015

page 95
"The world was my oyster but I used the wrong fork."
Oscar Wilde
The Protocol School of Washington
Psow.edu 23rd February 2015

page 105
"Don't reserve your best behavior for special occasions. You can't have two sets of manners, two social codes—one for those you admire and want to impress, another for those whom you consider unimportant. You must be the same to all people."
Lillian Eichler Watson
Famous Quotes and Quotations
Famousuotesandquotations.com 23rd February 2015

page 123
"There are three possible parts to a date, of which at least two must be offered: entertainment, food and affection. It is customary to begin a series of dates with a great deal of entertainment, a moderate amount of food, and the merest suggestion of affection. As the amount of affection increases, the entertainment can be reduced proportionately. When the affection IS the entertainment, we no
longer call it dating. Under no circumstances can the food be omitted."
Judith Martin
Goodreads.com 23rd February 2015

page 127

"However so much as you are capable of doing, dare to do that much."
Thomas Aquinas
Fr. Z's Blog Wdtprs.com 23rd February 2015

page 135

"I fear the day that technology will surpass our human interaction. The world will have a generation of idiots."
Unknown
Goodreads.com 23rd February 2015

page 151

"It is a wise thing to be polite; consequently, it is a stupid thing to be rude. To make enemies by unnecessary and wilful incivility, is just as insane a proceeding as to set your house on fire. For politeness is like a counter—an avowedly false coin, with which it is foolish to be stingy."
Arthur Schopenhauer
Counsels and Maxims From the Essays of Arthur Schopenhauer
Gutenburg.org 25th February 2015

page 159

"There is nothing noble about being superior to some other man. The true nobility is in being superior to your previous self."
Hindu Proverb
Gaiam Life
Blog.gaiam.com 25th February 2015

page 159
"Practice yourself in little things… and thence proceed to greater."
Epictetus
Philosiblog.com 25th February 2015

page 164
"Each of us must work for his own improvement, and at the same time share a general responsibility for all humanity."
Marie Curie
In Her Own Words: Secret Studies in Warsaw
aip.org 25th February 2015

page 167
"Kindness is a language which the deaf can hear and the blind can see."
Mark Twain
Charamission.org 25th February 2015

page 170
"Their manners are more gentle, kind, than of our generation you shall find."
William Shakespeare
The Tempest Books.google.com.au 25th February 2015

page 175
"Victory is in the quality of the competition and not the final score."
Mike Marshall
Smartbrief.com 25th February 2015

page 177

"It's a funny thing about life, if you refuse to accept anything but the best,
you very often get it."

Somerset Maugham

Wordreference.com

Forum.wordreference.com 25th February 2015

page 179

"Elegance is the only beauty that never fades."

Audrey Hepburn

"I Don't Do Fashion. I Am Fashion"—The 50 Best Style Quotes Of All
Time

Suzannah Ramsdale, December 23 2014

Marieclaire.co.uk 25th

February 2015

First published in 2017 by New Holland Publishers

London • Sydney • Auckland
The Chandlery 50 Westminster Bridge Road London SE1 7QY United Kingdom
1/66 Gibbes Street Chatswood NSW 2067 Australia
5/39 Woodside Ave Northcote, Auckland 0627 New Zealand

A record of this book is held at the British Library and the National
Library of Australia.

ISBN 9781742570143

Managing Director: Fiona Schultz
Publisher: Diane Ward
Project Editor: Anna Brett
Design: Lorena Susak
Proofreader: Kaitlyn Smith
Production Director: James Mills-Hicks

Printer: Hang Tai Printing Company Limited

10 9 8 7 6 5 4 3 2 1

Keep up with New Holland Publishers on Facebook
www.facebook.com/NewHollandPublishers